Beyond Control

*Managing Strategic Alignment
through Corporate Dialogue*

Beyond Control

Managing Strategic Alignment through Corporate Dialogue

Fred Lachotzki
Robert Noteboom

John Wiley & Sons, Ltd

Copyright © 2005   John Wiley & Sons Ltd, The Atrium, Southern Gate, Chichester,
West Sussex PO19 8SQ, England

Telephone   (+44) 1243 779777

Reprinted with corrections October 2006

Email (for orders and customer service enquiries): cs-books@wiley.co.uk
Visit our Home Page on www.wileyeurope.com or www.wiley.com

Other Wiley Editorial Offices

John Wiley & Sons Inc., 111 River Street, Hoboken, NJ 07030, USA

Jossey-Bass, 989 Market Street, San Francisco, CA 94103-1741, USA

Wiley-VCH Verlag GmbH, Boschstr. 12, D-69469 Weinheim, Germany

John Wiley & Sons Australia Ltd, 33 Park Road, Milton, Queensland 4064, Australia

John Wiley & Sons (Asia) Pte Ltd, 2 Clementi Loop #02-01, Jin Xing Distripark, Singapore 129809

John Wiley & Sons Canada Ltd, 22 Worcester Road, Etobicoke, Ontario, Canada M9W 1L1

Wiley also publishes its books in a variety of electronic formats. Some content that appears in print may not
be available in electronic books.

Library of Congress Cataloging-in-Publication Data

Lachotzki, Fred.
  Beyond control : managing strategic alignment through corporate dialogue
/ Fred Lachotzki & Robert Noteboom.
      p. cm.
  Includes bibliographical references and index.
  ISBN 0-470-01152-1 (cloth : alk. paper)
  1. Organizational change. 2. Strategic planning. 3. Communication in
management. 4. Leadership. 5. Industrial management. I. Noteboom,
Robert. II. Title.
  HD58.8.L313 2005
  658.4'5—dc22
2004018709

British Library Cataloguing in Publication Data

A catalogue record for this book is available from the British Library

ISBN10: 0-470-01152-1 (HB)   ISBN13: 978-0-470-01152-2 (HB)

Typeset in 11/13pt Goudy by Dobbie Typesetting Ltd, Tavistock, Devon
Printed and bound in Great Britain by TJ International Ltd, Padstow, Cornwall
This book is printed on acid-free paper responsibly manufactured from sustainable forestry
in which at least two trees are planted for each one used for paper production.

Contents

Introduction

In 2001, when various high-profile corporate scandals began to emerge, many journalists, educators and regulators jumped on the issue of failure and corporate governance. They viewed the apparent lack of transparency and accountability within organizations as the main cause of failure and/or fraud. In this book, we aim to show that transparency and accountability need not only be conspicuous negatively – that is, through their *absence* – but can in fact be the *positive* results of a modern management style and in this way transformed into real assets. And we are not only referring to transparency and accountability involving financial results, but also alignment between strategy and execution.

Throughout our 30 years of experience as, variously, manager, president, managing board member, consultant and nonexecutive director, we have continually struggled with certain classic leadership issues:

- How to align strategy and execution.
- How to create and sustain focus and energy in an organization.
- How to create a structure for involving talent without dissipating momentum.
- How to provide maximum freedom for key people without losing control.
- How to measure and manage the organization's overall capability.

We have learnt that the state of a company's Strategic Alignment is an effective indicator for future success and sustainable profitability. Therefore, a key point we wish to emphasize in this book is that *leadership* of large corporations should extend 'Beyond Control', through the implementation of a *system for strategic alignment* that complements the traditional management control systems.

The logic and approach of this book may be illustrated with a medical analogy. Part 1 describes the *symptoms* of the problem – the system failure – and offers a *diagnosis* by describing why there is a need to move beyond existing processes. Part II introduces the details of the *cure*: in our case, this is simultaneously the solution – a new management style – and the necessary set of tools to apply it. Finally, Part III examines the detailed administration of this cure to the patient by describing the roles and duties of the key people responsible for implementing *management beyond control*.

A new approach

Five years after starting our research efforts on the subject, this book presents a new leadership approach for the twenty-first century. Our research shows that leaders are able to inspire people, unlock corporate talent and build highly disciplined, competitive companies if they create an *operating arena* (the portfolio of the company's organizational capabilities) that enables people to work with *clear, responsible freedom*.

To be effective, such an operating arena requires a structured dialogue between the leader and key executives. Once created, such an arena allows you to both manage organizational capabilities and keep strategy and execution aligned, so that there is no gap between where the CEO wants the organization to go and where it is currently heading.

In leadership positions, including company president, we have chaired numerous corporate events and motivational sessions and endured endless travel. But even all this was never enough to ensure that the company strategy was communicated deep into the organization, understood, commented on, accepted and consistently executed over time. The sheer size and complexity of businesses, together with the time for dialogue demanded by intelligent managers, wouldn't allow this to be achieved.

As nonexecutive members of boards in Europe and the USA, we discussed strategy, acquisitions, budgets and quarterly results. We attended audit and compensation committees, and maybe once a year we touched on organizational issues. Yet it was very difficult to gain insight into the actual organizational capabilities, which in the end determine the future of the company. This lack of transparency often made us feel uncomfortable.

As professors of business policy, both of us taught strategy formulation as well as strategy execution. Ample theory was available on these subjects, but there was very little on issues like aligning strategy and execution and measuring organizational capability. Yet we felt a real need to reflect on, get to know about and find solutions for doing just that. More knowledge was required, and once developed we hoped to translate that knowledge into workable solutions.

We realized that we needed a solid model to allow delegation and decentralization, one that would be institutionalized within the organization and enable the leveraging of the talents of key people without losing management control.

Consequently, in order to create a comprehensive knowledge base, we started developing our own models to measure and manage the organization's operating arena. Therefore, in this book, we not only try to present a modern and, for some, new approach to managing larger organizations, but also to address the desired profile and leadership style of the CEO and his[1] leadership team. Certainly, leaders will be judged by their integrity, but also by what they achieve. So we discuss *execution*, making sure that the company *achieves* what it and its leadership stand for and desire.

The research base

A research and leadership support company founded in 1999 helped us turn theory into practice. Since 1999, MeyerMonitor has applied its proprietary research platforms to various projects, serving a number of large multinational companies.[2] Indeed, over the past five years, many of the different concepts in this book have been developed in association with these companies, which have served as a laboratory for the tools presented in the book.

We started by trying to measure organizational capability, but it soon became clear that measuring alone was not enough. Therefore, we developed further tools to help the process of dialogue, and to deepen our understanding of possible solutions for improving performance. At a later stage we felt the need for a more formalized dialogue. This led to the development of the *executive dialogue centre*, the portal at the core of our system of what we call 'pull and push' management.

Strategic pull and operational push

Creating involvement in a global corporation is a question of striking the right balance between allowing people freedom to create, innovate and make decisions on the one hand, and enforcing accountability, control, focus and prioritization on the other. Whereas management by objectives gives a company *strategic pull*, incorporating the implicit objectives and ideas of people deep within the organization will create *operational push* and build ownership of strategy and execution.

Our approach of *management beyond control* (described in more detail below) integrates strategic pull and operational push, stretching and strengthening the company's agility and resilience. In return, however, the CEO must be willing to give up a command-and-control mindset.

Strategic alignment and the corporate black box

It is essential that companies manage not only their results but also their alignment. This book is about aligning strategy and execution, which in turn requires structured, well-understood processes of managing the 'means' to reach the 'ends'. It is also about managing organizational capabilities to make the desired performance a reality.

Managing the 'means' requires managing the organizational capabilities. Unfortunately, due to the sheer size and complexity of their enterprises, many company leaders have felt forced to 'black box' their operations by putting the focus on achieving objectives rather than being actively involved in managing the organizational capabilities to meet those objectives.

Operating arena

In order to open up the black box, we introduce a system of management that we call *management beyond control*, which involves the creation of a highly stimulating, strategically aligned *operating arena* for the company's key executives, where not only financial results but also organizational capabilities are permanently *measured* and *managed*.

An aligned operating arena gives a company the capacity to execute by ensuring clarity about its strategic intent, creating compelling objectives, enabling permanent interaction and creating a supportive organization. The end-result will be high levels of transparency and accountability for all operating areas, not just financial results.

Corporate dialogue

Management beyond control takes place through *corporate dialogue*. The process of alignment through corporate dialogue results in an aligned operating arena. Corporate dialogue, in our definition, means measuring and managing a company's strategic alignment. It involves permanently aligning organizational capabilities with strategic initiatives by measuring the status of these capabilities, by creating a strategic alignment agenda – what we call the matching process – and by structured follow-through of organizational improvement initiatives.

The executive dialogue centre

For CEOs to reach out deep into their organizations and be better understood by their key people, and vice-versa, they need a modern alternative to 'management by walking around', which is impossible in a global company. A virtual CEO office or *executive dialogue centre* (EDC) is the answer. It can enable monthly motivation sessions and leverage the board's time, while also giving key executives structured access to the CEO's office to ask questions, provide input and stay strategically aligned. As a result, decisions will be more effective and supported.

Moving beyond control

After many years of intense research and the development and testing of solutions in real operating environments, we feel that we can offer a proven management approach that takes the modern CEO's leadership style 'beyond control' by focusing on a structured dialogue in the organization's operating arena. A well-defined operating arena makes it possible for CEOs to measure and manage strategic alignment. Measuring provides the ability to create transparency and make accountability a reality, even for hard-to-grasp, 'soft' areas.

We believe that every CEO, manager, board member and business student can gain something from this book. We hope that the examples and tool sets will stimulate action, but most of all we hope that the book will contribute towards thinking about the alignment of strategy and execution.

Although the book includes some theoretical background to our thinking, such as complexity theory and thoughts about freedom and fear, we did not try to write an extensively academic book on all theories and subjects in connection with strategic management, organizational dynamics and corporate design. There are enough good books available by more specialized authors on these specific subjects. We have tried to write a book that is easy to read and can help managers create better companies through pull and push management.

Making the best use of information and communications technology can help create companies where talent is involved, energy is focused, and strategy formulation and implementation are well aligned. In the twenty-first century there will be many more changes in how people communicate, work and play using digital devices of all kinds. These will have consequences for company structures and management styles. If we can contribute to creating better management systems by taking advantage of those changes, this gives us confidence that large organizations can be run both properly and more effectively.

Layout of the book

In Part 1, we discuss the mindset that has prevailed for the managing of large corporations over the past few decades. To this end, Chapter 1 gives several examples of misalignment between strategy and execution and tries to answer the question: why have so many leaders drifted away from the heart of their companies? Chapter 2 asks whether it was human failure, system failure or a combination of the two that caused so many things to go wrong. In order to answer that question and come up with a solution, we look back and see what we can learn from the past.

In order to re-position the CEO at the heart of the company – so that he can manage strategic alignment from the middle – we have to describe the managerial arena. Therefore, in Chapter 3 we define the *operating arena* as a portfolio of capabilities and discuss how to measure the quality of the arena. Chapter 4 then digs deeper into the leadership style that is most suited to *management beyond control*. We also examine the four factors that determine strategic alignment: the clarity of intent; the potency of objectives; the effectiveness of interaction; and the supportiveness of the organization.

In Part II, we discuss the actual process of *management beyond control*. Therefore, Chapter 5 defines *corporate dialogue* as measuring, matching and managing and we talk about the alignment agenda, which serves as the backbone for the alignment process. Chapter 6 then introduces the toolbox, the *Executive Dialogue Centre*, through which the process can be guided.

In Chapter 7, we discuss the theory supporting managing *beyond control*. The purpose of this chapter is to provide managers with a comfort level, some reassurance that this management style is based on well-researched principles.

Part III shows how the process can be embedded within the corporation. As *management beyond control* has to be put into practice by real people in the real world, Part III is arranged by the roles and responsibilities of the key players involved in this implementation.

The role of the *chief executive officer* (Chapter 8) is crucial because he spearheads the process of strategic alignment by inviting key executives to join in the dialogue and be involved in the creation of the company's alignment agenda. It is the CEO who enforces transparency and accountability for 'output' as well as 'throughput' data within the corporation.

The *chief financial officer*, whose responsibilities include the assessment and evaluation of the financial consequences of strategic decisions, also plays an important role in capturing all the data connected with the company's sustained profitability, including its organizational capability (Chapter 9). His role in the corporate dialogue extends to outside stakeholders through his ability to link financial figures with alignment data.

In most companies, it will be the *human resource director* who manages the operational 'push' (Chapter 10). Identifying the best talent for involvement in the process and following up key improvement projects are just two of this official's many tasks in a well-structured strategic alignment process.

The creation and maintenance of a coherent and consistent corporate 'story' is the prime responsibility of the *communications director* (Chapter 11). In most cases he will manage the operational side of the executive dialogue centre and, because of his professional expertise, will play an important role in keeping the agenda alive.

Throughout the chapters of Part III, we give suggestions on how to embed a system of *management beyond control* firmly within the company. Reward systems must be adjusted to reflect the fact that both financial and capability data are now combined to form assessments of the company's performance. Similarly, reporting systems must adjust, so that all stakeholders can be fully informed of those assessments and their separate financial and capability components.

Amsterdam, January 2005
F.L. and R.N.

HOW TO MANAGE
BEYOND CONTROL

... AND CREATE A STRATEGICALLY ALIGNED COMPANY

TAKE CHARGE

Ensure the strategic alignment process is measured
and managed as intensively as the financial results

BUILD THE INTERFACE

3 ACTIONS TO ALIGN EXECUTION WITH STRATEGY

measuring	matching	managing
INVOLVE KEY EXECUTIVES IN ASSESSING THE COMPANY CAPABILITIES	PRIORITIZE CAPABILITY IMPROVEMENTS TO ALIGN WITH STRATEGY	CREATE AN EXECUTIVE DIALOGUE CENTRE TO PERMANENTLY LEAD THE ALIGNMENT PROCESS

ACTIVATE THE SYSTEM

– MAKE THE ALIGNMENT PROCESS AN INTEGRAL PART OF THE
EXISTING STRATEGIC & BUDGETARY MANAGEMENT CYCLE
– REWARD EXECUTIVES ON THE BASIS OF FINANCIAL
RESULTS *AND* STRATEGIC ALIGNMENT

PUBLISH

VERIFY AND ANNOUNCE THE ACTUAL STATE OF
STRATEGIC ALIGNMENT IN THE ANNUAL REPORT

Acknowledgements

The suggestion that we write this book came from Harvard professor John Deighton. We are indebted to John for the many hours spent sparring with us and strengthening our thinking. The inspiration came from Maria Meyer, founder of MeyerMonitor; someone totally devoted to making sure that talented, committed people are recognized for their merits and fulfil their potential.

The input of Roland Kupers has been of the utmost importance. Managing beyond control is based on a belief in the validity of complexity theory, and the intense discussions we had on this subject have been key to developing the foundation of our thinking.

We owe gratitude to the many multinational companies MeyerMonitor has worked with over the last five years, for their assistance in the development of many of our concepts and for their service as a collective laboratory for the tools presented in this book.

We consider Transparency and Accountability crucial assets, and a vital ingredient towards their strengthening is Open-Mindedness. The fact that business leaders from companies such as TNT, ABN AMRO, Sara Lee/DE, Numico, Warner Lambert and Heineken so generously made available their capability survey results proves their commitment to the subject and to openness.

A special thank you goes to the three CEOs who spent long hours reading the manuscript at an early stage. Their detailed comments made us realize that we still had much work to do: Gerard Kleisterlee of Philips, Thony Ruys of Heineken and British Telecom's CEO Ben Verwaayen.

We have also received valuable suggestions from Dr. Bram Peper, former mayor of the city of Rotterdam and former Cabinet minister of the Netherlands; Dr. Otto von den Gablenz, former German ambassador to the Netherlands, Israel, and Russia; Dr. Kalun Tse, Professor of Corporate Finance at Nyenrode University; Peter Korsten, executive director of the IBM Institute of Business Value; Jos Nijhuis, Chairman of the PricewaterhouseCoopers Board in the Netherlands; Antony Burgmans, Chairman, Unilever N.V.; Dr. Hans Wijers, Chairman and CEO of Akzo Nobel; Karel Schellens, CEO of De Lage Landen International; Dr. Richard Jones; and Michael Moore.

All the members of the MeyerMonitor team have helped us to bring this book to completion. We want especially to thank Kai Grunewald, Robert Mol, Kiki De LiguoriCarino, Job van Harmelen, Nicole Messer and Jeroen Hilberts.

Inspiration also came from Hans van Meer, Fred's long-time mentor during the 1970s and 1980s, from Peter van Dun and Willem Stevens, Professor Pedro Nueno of IESE Business School, as well as from faculty colleagues at Nyenrode University, in particular Dr. Fred van Eenennaam and our many graduate students. Enduring encouragement came from long-time friend Xander van Meerwijk and from Neelie Kroes, former President of Nyenrode University.

Finally, without the editing help of Andy Finch, Sally Lansdell, Maria Meyer and Michael A. Olson, this book would never have emerged into the light of day. We would like to thank them, together with the Wiley team.

Part I

Moving Beyond Control
A New Concept

In Part I, we discuss the mindset that has prevailed for the managing of large corporations over the past decades. We also introduce our equation for sustained profitability, which clarifies why a new concept for managing *beyond control* is needed, and how this is best achieved.

I

Strategic Alignment: Is a New System Needed?

Companies should be able to endure and grow far beyond the lifetime of individual CEOs. Endurance requires more than a few years of excellent financial results. It demands strategic alignment. In this chapter, we examine why so many large companies during the last decades have had trouble aligning their execution with the board's strategic initiatives. Why have so many leaders drifted away from the heart of their companies? What has gone wrong?

Opening up the operational 'black box' is a first step towards achieving corporate dialogue, transparency and accountability.

The profitability equation

Sustainable profit is realized when a business possesses the core competencies to outperform its industry peers because of a unique value proposition and/or operational excellence. A leadership team's responsibility is to conduct its business so that direction and execution are aligned, monitored and followed over time.

There should be the right mixture of key performance indicators, oriented both to organizational capability as well as to profitability, where relatively short-term investments and results are balanced with longer-term aspects. Managers should be held accountable not only for financial results, but also for the creation of support systems that enable their subordinates to excel. This approach will lead to greater checks and balances, and will have the potential to create a more stable flow of profits.

Sustained profitability = Financial results x Strategic alignment

The antithesis of this equation is represented by all those companies – e.g. Enron, Tyco, Ahold, Parmalat – that have been so well publicized in the last few years after they were 'suddenly' hit by bad results. It turned out that they had no infrastructure in place to manage their fast growth in a sound way.

Several quarters and even years of great financial results x bad strategic alignment = lack of sustained profitability

Companies like these go out of control because they lack sufficient strategic alignment.

A company can create the necessary level of stability by sharing with its most important stakeholders the status of all parts of the equation – including its continual efforts to strengthen its organizational capability. Regularly sharing such data with analysts who are following the company might also help to create a discussion that is focused more on the long term than just on the following quarter. Once a corporation becomes appreciated for these more fundamental investments in its future, it is half way to creating sustainable profits.

Moving beyond control

We need a model that is based on the right set of indicators to reassure managers that they are in control. What is required is the kind of control over the corporation that does not restrict people or create bureaucratic obstacles. We need a system that can be managed 'beyond control'.

How things can go out of control

Reflecting on 30 years in business and academia, one of the authors (Fred) is quite willing to admit that he focused too much on operational outcomes. If, instead, the alignment between strategy and execution had been managed, and if today's technology and knowledge had been available, several of the instruments that we will discuss in this book could have been used. Although successes were celebrated, Fred also faced disappointments. Quite a few of the mistakes, inefficiencies, failed experiments and integrity issues encountered in his career could have been avoided.

Fred will now describe four examples from his career, first to illustrate the kind of problems to which we are referring and second to show how creating strategic alignment through corporate dialogue could have helped. In one or two examples, for reasons of discretion, certain parts of the description have been changed.

The liquor store

Early in my career I was running a small but fast-growing chain of liquor stores, which at the time had 40 outlets. We had introduced a private-label Campari equivalent, called Campagne Amari, the label for which read almost like Campari. Campari sued us. We lost the case and the court ordered us to pay a large amount of money for any bottle found after a specific date set in the near future.

As I was about to attend Harvard's Program for Management Development for four months and was scheduled to leave Europe a week after the court's decision, I directed the operational manager (following the normal hierarchical structure) to make sure that there wouldn't be any bottles on the shelves after the designated date. In addition, I wrote an instruction in our weekly information bulletin for the stores. Then I left for Boston.

What happened? Several bottles were found in a particular store after the designated date. The amount we had to pay was so much that we lost more than half our profit for that year.

The restaurant experiment

Managing a restaurant division was my next assignment and during my time there we wanted to test some new concepts.

One was the idea of sophisticated pancakes in one of the high streets of downtown Amsterdam. In addition to sweet crêpes, the idea was to offer main-meal crêpes stuffed with fish, meat or vegetables. The profitability of a restaurant is very much dependent on the gross profit per table and so having main meals was important. You need a high average bill and quick table turnover. The whole concept was conceived at company headquarters and investment was duly allocated. Fortunately, a good location was available: a high-street restaurant that our company had run for more than 25 years, but which for the last few years had been losing money. It had a very old clientele, who came in for coffee and cake.

We remodelled the restaurant and immediately noticed that it was well occupied. Nevertheless, at the end of the first week sales were low, and they didn't improve in the second, third or fourth week. We found this strange because the restaurant was always full of people. Shortly afterwards we ended the experiment and sold the building to avoid losing more money.

The faraway supermarket

As a newly appointed management board member of a large German retail firm, I was asked to be our liaison with a supermarket chain that we owned 50/50 with another German retailer. This chain, which operated in the southern United States, had a mostly German management team and a positive bottom-line: it had recently acquired a large group of stores from another chain, had opened some very large new stores, and was considered to be extremely successful. I decided to travel to the US and visit at least 60% of the stores (about 75), including all those that had opened during the previous three years. Up to that point, the supermarket chain had been supervised mainly by four board meetings a year during which board members were shown around selected stores.

My first three weeks were interesting. The language of the management team was mainly German, not English. Several (very dusty) German products were to be found on the supermarket shelves. Although the new stores were extremely pleasant and luxurious, they had few customers. The real estate of several stores had recently been sold to investors (i.e. asset profits had been generated) and then rented back. I returned to Germany upset and worried. After a period of hard work, some firing and repositioning, the company was sold.

The nonexecutive board member

One of the boards I sat on was that of a fast-growing company operating in many countries around the world. The board was presented with a strategic agenda built around an aggressive acquisition programme, supplemented by autonomous growth through existing and new clients. The managing members of the board convinced us that the acquisitions would be in related businesses. A key argument was that one-stop shopping would create large synergies. We would acquire companies whose offerings could be added to ours and consequently offered to the existing client base.

Two years later we missed profit targets several quarters in a row, our stock had fallen sharply, and shortly thereafter we divested most of our acquisitions.

How problems were caused by the operations being 'black boxed'

Let's have another look at these four real-life cases. Could money have been saved, embarrassment avoided or failing experiments stopped earlier?

The liquor store

In this case the strategy was clear: consolidating the retail liquor market by applying a discount concept while making money. When I returned from the US, my boss on the board asked if I had learned the lesson: that an effective executive knows his priorities – when to go into detail and when not to. With such potentially large losses at stake, I should not have followed the regular hierarchy, but instead had a direct dialogue with store managers.

I should have put myself in the middle of the operation and taken the time to call every store manager personally and have them check whether any bottles were present in the stores. The smallish size of the company made that possible. Of course, if electronic digital communication had been available, it would have taken me no more than half an hour to notify everyone. So it was a question of experience and scope/time. Did things go wrong because I had put the store operation into a black box, accessible by the operational boss but not by me?

The restaurant experiment

In the second case, the problem was that the marketing concept was developed centrally. We kept the strategy for the concept close to our chests (for security reasons). The crucial fact was that we needed an average bill per table that could only be reached if a high percentage of customers ordered a full meal (i.e. dinner crêpes) and if the average seating time did not exceed 45 minutes. Only later did we discover that the old clientele usually stayed in the restaurant for an average of one hour and fifteen minutes and mostly only ordered coffee. People who had worked at store level knew this, but because they were unaware of our assumptions and agenda they could not warn us in advance.

Possibly the company lacked a 'listening' culture and structure. The leadership team was so convinced and enthusiastic about the new concept that operations may have thought it better to keep quiet and avoid irritating the leadership – and in any case we might not have wanted to hear what they had to say. We also later found out that after the new restaurant had been open for two days, the store manager noticed that almost all his old customers were visiting and staying for two hours with just coffee and one simple sweet crêpe. As he didn't know our strategic agenda (average bill, seating time), he didn't report this to us. When I visited the location during the first few days, I saw only a full restaurant.

If we had shared the agenda with more key people, the difficulty of meeting the goal for the average bill might have come out into the open much earlier. If we had had a culture where people were used to giving input or critically addressing marketing issues with the leadership, we might at least have given them the opportunity to react more quickly. In this situation we didn't take any action until the company's controller had done the analysis two months later, which was too late. Again, the operation was too much of a black box.

The faraway supermarket

The third example was a large company with divisions run as separate businesses by 'independent' executives operating in a different culture far away from headquarters. The objectives were clear (mainly financial), board meetings were about financial budgets and held a maximum of four times a year (often less), and local management staged store visits. It turned out that executives were not sensitive enough to the culture, and that there were issues of integrity in both financial and purchasing decisions: for instance, real-estate profits were mixed with operational results. There was an evident problem of marketing competence (the wrong size and wrong type of store), and all this was concealed from the German headquarters.

If there had been an open dialogue throughout the organization, managers could have questioned store concepts and raised issues of store size and investments, and employees might have pointed out the integrity issues. These were only some of the aspects that would have come up if there had been a regular dialogue and a clearly understood agenda, as well as shared objectives. If everything had been transparent and people accountable for the creation of a really supportive organization, how different matters would have been. Once again, we had simply black boxed this international operation.

The nonexecutive board member

The fourth case was about supervision. Many had been added to the group within just two years, some in the same industry, some in slightly related industries. Some were small, some large. Some were in the home country, some far away. Most were bought from entrepreneurs and although some were quite profitable, others weren't. Some were bought with stock, others for cash or a combination of cash and stock. Several were acquired with an earn-out provision[1]. But all these companies required management attention as, due to strong growth, did the existing operations to an ever-greater degree. The anticipated one-stop shopping, however, was not really taking place.

Most of the acquired companies were underperforming by the second year. After the management teams of the acquired companies had taken their earn-outs and left, we stepped in and were faced with some terrible surprises. Only after we had fired our CEO and CFO and read the report of the consultant we had hired to analyse the strategy did we realize that one-stop shopping had not materialized. It turned out that many managers deep in the organization knew that it would not work. They had talked about this, but it had never reached the board. Or had the CEO heard it but left us in the dark?

Furthermore, it emerged that managers had been afraid of the CEO. People had complained about his top-down budgeting style as well as his inaccessibility. In addition, the growth targets, stringent budgets and many acquisitions had asked too much of the organization's resilience. Fortunately, not all was bad. The core business had a willing market and a good reputation.

If over time we had developed structured, quantitative insight into the organizational capabilities of the corporation, including the acquired companies, wouldn't we have reduced the number of companies we bought? If there had been a structured (anonymous) internal dialogue between key people and the company's leadership

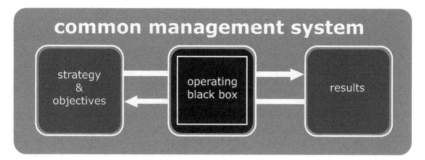

Figure 1.1 The operating black box

team, wouldn't the one-stop shopping idea have been challenged more strongly? Were we just hoping for good results to emerge out of the black box? (See Figure 1.1).

Opening up the black box

It is every CEO's nightmare to wake up in the middle of the night agonized by fear of failure, fear of not being in control, fear of losing his grip, fear of shattering his reputation. CEOs realize all too well that they need to have a sufficient understanding of what is happening behind the figures that their subordinates deliver to them.

Leaders expect that the managers reporting to them are allocating enough resources to create and support an effective infrastructure of the business unit they are running. But many are not always certain that this is the case. They expect that their subordinates are not destroying established customer, partner or employee relationships. Certainly they expect that their factories do not needlessly damage the environment – but how can they be sure?

Despite their expectations, leaders still notice divisions not performing to standard, market share slipping, talent leaving and some acquisitions not performing. They appreciate how important it is to have a deep understanding of the industry, to not be dependent on anecdotes, truly to see the whole reality of the firm, and to have a deep insight into the company's overall performance.

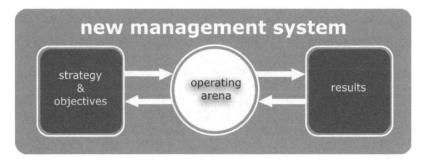

Figure 1.2 A new management system

They are painfully aware that to manage you need to measure more than merely financial objectives. Leaders realize that in order to operate in a perfectly transparent and accountable way, they have to open up the organizational black box and find a better way to measure and manage strategic alignment as well as financial results. They are in need of a different approach: a new management system (Figure 1.2). But, first, we need to understand the recent history of corporate development – how did we arrive at the current state of affairs?

Lessons learned

- Sustainable profits are a function of financial results and strategic alignment. Companies that have shown excellent financial results for many quarters in a row will not be sustainably profitable in the long run unless they are able to manage their strategic alignment.
- A common control system of checks and balances and formal verification by auditors may not be sufficient in itself to guarantee the level of transparency and accountability required so that one can judge a company's likely future success.
- Principles of transparency and accountability need to be closely defined, translated into measurable indicators and measured over time.
- Too much focus on management by objectives creates a tendency to 'black box' core business operations.

2

The Corporate Black Box: Understanding History

All managers and executives have made mistakes, and some have even been involved in corporate failures. And, of course, it is always easy to identify mistakes with the benefit of hindsight. We all do what we feel is best with the information we have at the time. Nevertheless, we always want to find better ways to manage. But before we can build a solid foundation for redefining a management approach that involves our talented people, we need a grasp of history.

We want to understand how cases like Enron and Ahold could arise to blight the successes of the last 40 years. Was it a question of human failure, system failure or a combination of the two? Or were the shortcomings merely part of a learning process about how to run and govern ever-larger enterprises? This chapter examines how corporations have developed over the past few decades.

Looking back

There have been such radical changes in the business environment in the last few years that we tend to forget where we started.[1] In the booming post-war years and throughout the late 1960s, the industrial landscape was quite uniform. What were its key features?

- Corporations concentrated on their home markets, where they found the majority of their revenue. Of course, there were global companies like General Motors, Ford, Unilever, Shell and Philips, but most companies focused close to home.
- Corporate governance was rarely discussed. Outside directors were selected on the basis of their experience, and sometimes because of their relationship with the company's chairman.
- In the US and UK, the positions of chairman and CEO were embodied in one and the same executive, who was in charge for many consecutive years. If the chairman or CEO was not a founder or from the family of founders, he – very rarely she – mostly came up through the company ranks. At the very least, usually he came from the industry in which the company was operating.
- Shareholders were considered important in the US and UK, but as long as they received an acceptable return on their capital through a combination of dividends and share price increase, everything was seen to be OK. In most other countries, shareholders were viewed merely as providers of capital, and played a very modest role. Most balance sheets were quite conservative, and assets were often undervalued, as they were put on the balance sheet at the original buying price or value, minus depreciation. Intellectual capital was hardly ever valued.
- Of course there were acquisitions, but most of them were reasonably friendly. The acquired company often possessed some undervalued assets in its balance sheet. In most cases, some of the executives of the acquired company joined the board of the combined company and integration was led from the top.
- In order to be competitive, corporations assumed that as many functions as possible should be brought together under a single management team. This integration would lead to maximum efficiency and the lowest possible price.
- Companies concentrated on establishing core competencies in their respective fields, had their own specialized research facilities and invested in corporate identities and brands. Their executives realized that they could exercise power over consumers as long as they controlled distribution channels and the superior image of their brands.

- The vogue in the 1960s and 1970s for ever-larger conglomerates ultimately revealed (with only a few exceptions) that managing companies in different industries under one umbrella does not bring success.
- Employees, middle managers and specialists alike had a relationship of dependency with their company. Companies owned the means of production, without which employees could not make a living. This meant that the employee was much more dependent on the corporation than the other way round. Most employees and managers had no more than one or two employers during their working life.

Companies in the 1980s and 1990s

At the end of the 1960s, the situation started to change. This was reflected in the work of academics who were starting to study the functioning of corporations, the role of management, the possibilities of corporate finance and so on. The 'profession' of corporate management was developing, particularly in the US.

Shareholders were becoming more demanding, and managers were coming under pressure to perform and use their available resources to produce better results.

In the 1980s and 1990s, the first corporate raiders emerged; these started to look at the market capitalization of companies and to compare that with their break-up value. Similarly, executives looked at the balance sheets of their competitors; if they discerned an undervalued company, they considered a hostile takeover.

Furthermore, managers and academics alike realized that fully integrated corporations were not functioning optimally. There were two reasons for this. First, knowledge about specialized areas was difficult to obtain; because companies consequently missed out on economies of scale in these areas, their operations became too costly. Second, because of developments in information technology the physical cost of communication was vastly reduced and activities could be outsourced quite easily. For example, companies could now shift their computer centre to a continent 10 000 miles away.

Another phenomenon was that knowledge became a means of production. The business world started talking about human capital in addition to physical capital. Companies began to realize that they were as dependent on their key people for survival as employees were dependent on the company for their income. This led to the colourful expression that a company's most important assets walk out the door every evening.

The next change was in the company's relationship with its customer base. Until the 1970s most of the power was in the hands of the corporation. In the business-to-business environment as much as in the consumer market, customers relied heavily on companies' brands and distribution networks.

In the 1990s, the Internet drastically changed the ground-rules. Some industrial customers auctioned off their demand based on well-defined specifications and gave their business to the lowest bidder, wherever this bidder originated. Old client/supplier relationships founded on many years of collaboration and personal investment by both parties simply fell away. The upshot has been that consumers have gained more and more power; in many areas manufacturers have ceased to be mere sellers and have become buyers for customers instead.

Digitization transformed whole business models. Companies like Google, Amazon and computer manufacturer Dell demonstrated that the product as such is no longer the key to corporate success. Companies started competing with new business models designed for efficiency and perfection in such areas as logistics and the customer relationship. The business model *was* the product. Furthermore, it became apparent that it was possible to sell more than just the original product lines through the same system. Think of Amazon's expansion from books into CDs, computer games and even healthcare; or the mobile phone companies' transformation into providers of much wider entertainment and information services; or Yahoo's expansion from search engine to email provider to software developer. Suddenly ownership of the traditional supply chain, in which large amounts of time, money and the building and maintaining of relationships had been invested, became a much less-significant asset.

Short-term shareholder expectations

During the 1990s, Wall Street became king: more companies were driven by their share price than ever before. Share prices are strongly determined by profit growth expectations, so some CEOs concluded that it was better to listen to the analysts commenting on the company than to the executives operating it. It became axiomatic that the only person able to disturb a CEO in the middle of his regular Monday-morning management board meeting was the lead analyst covering his company. When this person asked to speak to the CEO, the number one would interrupt his meeting, take the call and listen to the investment bank representative. No customer and no manager inside the company had the power to do that. Outperforming your industry peers on Wall Street instead of Main Street became the name of the game.

The fixation on the share price had all kinds of causes. Some resembled a vicious circle. You needed growth, which meant takeovers. Takeovers could be achieved, at least in many cases, wholly or partly with stock. A high share price made such takeovers easier and therefore growth faster. On the other hand, a high share price meant protection from acquisitions by others; it also meant that there was more value in the stock options. Stock options were issued to attract talented people; a growth in the stock price meant that not only the CEO and his leadership team became rich (at least on paper) but so did the company's key talent. And so on and so on.

Everyone was focused on share price growth. CEOs started making claims about the next few quarters instead of merely the next one. Missing one or two quarters meant heavy punishment, in the form of a fall in the company's share price.

Growing complexity

The global scale of management and the speed of change certainly had their impact, but this was only gradual. A more fundamental change lay in the vast increase in interconnections and the exceptional growth in knowledge content that was needed in order to map out everything that went on. It became exceedingly difficult to reconstruct the causal chain that led to many events.

An example was the systemic collapse of the agricultural industry caused by the outbreak of foot-and-mouth disease in the UK at the beginning of the twenty-first century. This led to much finger-pointing. What was the cause of this bloody and expensive scandal? Was it the farmers' refusal to abide by the prohibition on moving their livestock, which spread the disease? Was it the systematic degradation of the livestock's genetic diversity, or the difficulty for policy makers of anticipating changes in the food system and enforcing controls? The high degree of interconnections and the systemic nature of the issue meant that no single accepted cause emerged from the public debate. Such issues defy our seemingly innate need for a 'simple' explanation of why things happen.

If we direct the discussion to the corporate world and look at the crises and apparent loss of control in several big corporations, again we can point the finger at various causes, without being sure that any one of them was truly key:

- Was it a question of too much ambition or too rapid expenditure?
- Did some companies expand beyond their own cultures in too short a time?
- Was it the fact that a particular company did not have enough knowledge about cultural differences and business practices?
- Was the cause that some of these corporations appointed CEOs who were not from the same industry and therefore lacked the necessary experience and 'feeling' for the job?
- Or was it the fact that the new generation of managers were operating with a different attitude than their older colleagues, who had been educated 15 years earlier under different norms and with a different approach?
- Should we look at it from a purely knowledge-based point of view: was it that some of the newly appointed specialists were using such sophisticated methods that the older generation did not understand things any more?

- Did the drive for efficiency and digitization conflict with the call for innovation?
- Or was it personality?

After studying 51 companies that stumbled, Dartmouth professor of management Sydney Finkelstein identified the pathologies that encourage CEOs to tilt towards recklessness.[2] Among them were underestimating obstacles, obsession with image, blatant attention seeking and identifying so completely with the company that they treat it like a personal fiefdom.

However, we cannot extract from this any single explanation. In some cases it might have been caused by the individual CEO; in others it could have been the sheer size of the company in combination with the speed of change. We have to draw the conclusion that events and circumstances were so interconnected that they were extremely difficult to identify individually.

Companies tried to deal with the multiple dimensions of their business by using different approaches. Some constructed two- or three-dimensional matrix organizations to address the different drivers. More recently, swaying with the tide of management wisdom, many have abandoned these again, but seemingly only on the organization charts: the underlying reality has not been put back into the bottle of simplicity.

In some cases the solution to tackling increased complexity was more or less to ignore it. If growth was the primary motto and you felt the pressure quarter after quarter to meet Wall Street's expectations, you might have been tempted to look the other way. There just wasn't enough time – not enough time for reflection; not enough time to take off with your leadership team for a few days to question some of the assumptions made a few years earlier about your businesses. These assumptions could be about world politics, exchange rates, cultural changes, ethics and business principles in general; or about the industry, competition, substitutes, key success factors, the portfolio of businesses and the strategic positioning that these businesses have chosen in the past; or about synergy, leadership, succession, customer relationships, unions, different governments and so on.

If there was not enough time to analyse these aspects and their interdependencies and draw suitable conclusions, the consequence was that lower-echelon managers were also left in the dark and forced to ignore it all. One way out has always been to simplify everything. Unfortunately, too many companies are still putting everything into the black box.

Leaders in the 1990s

Typically, the leaders running the new corporations were educated in the environment of the late 1960s. Many of these CEOs were more or less self-made, did not come from established families, and in several cases were considered celebrities by the outside world – and sometimes also by themselves. Boards awarded these leaders large share option packages, which made several of them extremely wealthy indeed. Their successful careers were based on a mindset strongly focused on management by objectives. 'If you can't dream it, you can't do it', was their mantra. Follow the market, look for opportunities, check the numbers and profit will appear.

But as we have seen, times had changed. Now these leaders had to operate in new markets, in different companies and sometimes even in different industries from those in which they had learned their trade, and they were no longer always able to look behind the numbers. Unlike the previous generation, the new-generation MBAs these leaders hired did not merely follow orders. They used different techniques, had different business principles, and in many cases came from different cultures – they were just plain different. In the meantime, business models were changing, shareholders were becoming more demanding and a new kind of interdependency was unfolding. Alliances were forming and managers were expected to work in company cultures based on meritocracy, knowledge sharing and respect.

A loss of transparency and accountability

Another characteristic of the recent business environment has been a loss of transparency and accountability. This is despite the fact that in most western societies people consider transparency and accountability to be fundamental principles that we should all live by as citizens, employees, politicians and executives. These principles are closely related to integrity, which should be the foundation of everything we do:

- Companies must be built around customers' priorities if they want to survive. This means that they should deliver what they promise – which is a question of integrity.
- If companies want to survive they should not destroy their environment. They should be as responsible as they claim to be – which is a question of integrity.
- If talented people are promised career development, the organization has to stand by its word – which is a question of integrity.

We could go on and on.

Nevertheless, during the last few decades we have needed consumer activists to pursue customer complaints and environmental activists to take our oil companies to task. We have needed government prosecutors to go after some of our accounting firms. We thought we could trust our products; we thought companies would act like responsible citizens; we thought we could rely on our annual reports; and we thought that if we were hired and promised support and personal development we would get it. There has been disappointment at all levels.

Now we demand transparency before we sign up for a new job, or invest in a company, or allow a factory to be built or products to be offered. We want to know who is responsible when things go wrong. Even better, we want to know where the accountability is *before* things go wrong. Corporations have become so big, and often so bureaucratic, that too many boards are far away from the average employee, shareholder or citizen. In too many cases we have lost both transparency and accountability.

Transparency

Internal

Within companies it has become more and more apparent that knowledge sharing, clarity of decisions and bottom-up communication are significant challenges. Our research clearly indicates that the biggest gap between what managers want and what they have to deal with is in the transparency of decision making and communication.[3] That goes for every industry, every culture and almost every company.

This is not so illogical if we take account of the fact that in the 1990s companies were growing fast and having to integrate acquisitions and change computer systems several times, all within a few years. They were streamlining processes, going digital, starting to use the Internet and having to cope with the enormous pressure to show financial results. It would not have been unlikely for a CEO to tell his divisional managers: 'We need another $10 million profit this quarter'. He might not have been fully interested in the details as long as the results were delivered. If they weren't, he could always replace the old manager and find a better one.

More or less the same was happening in the relationship between some senior managers and their outside directors. Partly driven by the fact that there was too little time to think deeply about what key performance indicators should be used to supervise the company over the long run, managers and directors tended to concentrate mostly on financial indicators. What lay behind the figures was either rarely, or never, discussed because of a lack of time. In a period of growth, and with CEOs who also chaired boards – or, on a two-tier board, CEOs who had extremely strong characters and therefore more or less ruled the meetings – not enough people forced more internal transparency.

Nowadays, both internal and external key stakeholders seek insight into the real quality of the company's leadership. Is its management board really meeting every week and for how long? Who is present on a formal basis and who chairs these meetings? Transparency about the actual behaviour of the CEO and his board often provides a better insight into the status of the company than data coming out of the annual report.

External

Take a company with tens of thousands of people operating in many countries with millions of customers, hundreds of suppliers and many governments with which it must deal – how can it ensure transparency? And transparency about what in particular? Market position, organizational capabilities, customer satisfaction, employee engagement, environmental policy or business practices in general? Where should it start being transparent and where should it stop?

Accountability

Internal

The typical company's combination of black boxing and management by (financial) objectives could lead one to think that managers are only held accountable for bottom-line performance. How they get to that performance, as we have argued above, might be seen as of lesser importance. It is hoped that they stay within the law (although, unfortunately, that hasn't always been the case), but what we judge them on is their financial results. We know that reputation, engagement, innovation and many more important drivers of future performance should be managed – but why measure them when, in the final analysis, the bottom line is all that counts?

But we should not forget that a company is a *value-creating* organism: organism because it consists of people, and value-creating because it creates – or at least should create – value. It creates shareholder value, customer value, employee value and societal value, to name but four, and in order to realize all of these objectives, managers need to create structural value. They have to invest in the firm's organizational capability. Managers should be held accountable for all of these value aspects.

Unfortunately, many firms have had a tendency to concentrate too much on financial accountability, and have introduced reward systems that accommodate this approach. You might say that remuneration packages and the stock options within them have led many companies to make a 'pact with the devil', namely accommodating Wall Street's short-term expectations and neglecting the need to manage complexity.

External

In many parts of the world, companies have been held accountable by shareholders for their financial performance, by communities for their creation of jobs, by suppliers for their solvency, by incoming talent for their career opportunities, by customers for the quality of their products and services, and by various pressure groups for their behaviour in society. But who has the real power to hold a company accountable? Stakeholders can only take action if they can identify measurable discrepancies.

Shareholders and their representatives are always in an easier position because the financial bottom-line is quite visible. In 2004, various investor activists forced the chairman of oil giant Shell to leave, stopped an expensive acquisition by mobile phone company Vodafone and stripped Michael Eisner, Disney's CEO, of his role as chairman. Customers can switch and talent can leave but how many of these other stakeholders have well-defined key performance indicators (other than financial ones) that can influence management appointments or rewards? We aren't arguing that they should necessarily have this information, but rather that somebody else (the board?) should take over the judgement on their behalf and keep the company accountable.

Strategy and execution

In the past, based on its competencies, the typical corporation grew by developing new products and opening new markets. As it grew in size, it added support functions and formed business units. In order to monitor what was happening, country managers were appointed and information systems installed. Delegation of responsibilities was necessary because it seemed unrealistic to steer a large company from only one place in the world. Accounting systems provided the data, and it was common practice for management boards to look at the results, compare them with the available two- or three-year plans, and approve or reject them. The last thing they did was get involved in the details or listen to any anecdotes that might reach them through the grapevine.

What was the aim of a typical corporation? It tried to deliver the best possible products and services at prices lower than the competition and at the lowest possible cost for its targeted customer groups. With this in mind, corporations tended to focus mostly on defining corporate financial targets, investment relations, acquisitions, the appointment of senior managers and incidental trouble-shooting.

Strategy discussions were about strategic choices of markets, acquisitions and investments. Execution was left up to the individual business units and involved discipline, leadership, motivation and a close watch on both customers and the competition.

Based on successful examples from the last 20 years, we can draw some conclusions about the best model for approaching corporate strategy and aligning strategy with execution. Corporations organized as a portfolio of businesses (for example the conglomerate GE) did quite well with an approach of delegation and management by objectives, as long as it was executed with discipline and competence and supported by corporate values. GE combined strategic initiatives that had to be carried out throughout the corporation with excellent financial systems. Business unit managers were free to run their own business in the way they wanted, guided by the strategic initiatives, but managers also knew that when some divisions were experiencing 'heavy weather', others should compensate. Ultimately, if an industry did not have the fundamental capability to achieve the right return on capital (such as the consumer electronics sector) or growth potential, GE left that industry.

We have seen companies, such as computer software giant Microsoft, change an industry and be very successful in the process. However, bigger corporations have realized their growth by trying to stay more or less within an industry they knew. Examples include Unilever, Nestlé, Procter & Gamble and Sara Lee in fast-moving consumer goods; Carrefour and Wal-Mart in retailing; and Delta, British Airways, Southwest Airlines and Air France in the airline industry. Each of these companies had to develop its own corporate structure, formulate a good strategy, and align the execution of that strategy in order to try and guarantee long-term sustainable profits.

Strategy is about selecting markets with the right customer groups and with the best profit potential, and formulating a unique value proposition based on the company's strength and core competencies on the one hand and operational efficiency on the other. We might assume that, with the appropriate organization, managers would be able to execute the defined strategy. Nevertheless, we have seen many examples in many industries where professional executives followed established procedures in a disciplined way and yet still failed to realize acceptable profit levels. A few examples follow:

- Many airlines were not able to match Southwest's performance. Several lost their independence or are not even in business anymore, including some that no one could imagine going bankrupt, such as PanAm, TWA or Swissair.
- Large retail companies like K-Mart and Ahold suddenly showed that their execution had failed: either they had overplayed their growth and/or there had been a misalignment between their strategic ambition and their executional capabilities.
- Dell Computer and Compaq are in the same industry and offer similar products. Dell competes with a digitized business model; Compaq competed with products. Dell leads the industry and has steadily gained market share while maintaining strong margins; Compaq lost its independence.

If we look at companies like Southwest Airlines and Dell, there is an interesting similarity. These companies have a business model that fully integrates their different activities based on a clear strategic positioning, while using their resources so efficiently that they are beating 'traditional' companies operating in their industry.

It seems that their executional capability fits their strategic positioning. But why have so many corporations not found the right alignment? Is the solution merely a 'simple', straightforward business model?

Could it be that successful companies started off the right way, with the right mindset, business model and management system? Is success only possible for companies that are able to operate with the above approach from the start?

Are existing large players never perfectly aligned because the traditional organizational model – whether matrix-, business line- or product group-based – is obsolete? Do size and lack of simplicity inevitably lead to misalignment between strategy and execution?

Signs of fraud

Throughout the centuries, we have seen administrators in both government and trade being punished for wrongdoing or corruption. Machiavelli, writing in the fifteenth century, pointed out how vulnerable leaders were to flattery and how power had a tendency to corrupt. Nothing has really changed. In our age, we have again been confronted with the fact that even in big public companies, overseen by CEOs or chairmen fully in the limelight and surrounded by well-respected outside directors, fraud can reach huge dimensions.

In the spring of 2001, BusinessWeek celebrated Tyco as one of the best-performing companies in the year 2000.[4] Over the previous three years, the company's stock had returned 117%, including a 44% return in 2000. The magazine concluded that 'its chairman knows how to navigate in rough waters. He had been readying Tyco for tougher times.' Tougher times did indeed come, but not in the way Tyco's stakeholders had foreseen. Misuse of funds and a whole range of examples of abuse of power suddenly came out into the open. The stock dropped dramatically; the chairman stepped down and has been put on trial.

As another example, Healthsouth Corp. fired its chairman in March 2002, after the FBI confirmed that it had been investigating whether he may have established offshore bank accounts the year before to avoid paying tax.

Boards under pressure

In the wake of company failures, their boards started to come under the microscope. Articles began to appear about problems in corporate governance on both sides of the Atlantic, and it made no difference whether a one-tier or two-tier board was involved. Some blamed the board members' lack of independence, as they were sitting on one another's boards; others blamed their lack of time, as many had seats on too many boards. Lack of independence was also an argument that appeared in countries where the company's bankers were on the board, and so on. Academics argued for a whole new system, as they felt that if the structural problems were not addressed, there would never be lasting improvement.[5]

Accountancy principles disputed

The fall of the accountancy firm Arthur Andersen in 2002 is also emblematic of systemic failure. It seems that the rules, regulations and principles of accountancy are in no way protecting the public against fraud or mismanagement. Accountancy firms themselves are not immune to unethical behaviour. As Barbara Toffler mentioned in her book *Final Accounting: Ambition, Greed, and the Fall of Arthur Andersen*, 'Andersen was dedicated to "Billing Our Brains Out"'. She worked at the firm from late 1995 to September 1999 and partners told her to drive up her billings, even if these were unjustified.

A major area of concern is the viability of company accounts. For instance, what about the costs of share options – shouldn't they be visible, or in fact subtracted from the results shown? As another example, if companies sell real estate and lease it back, shouldn't this be transparent, rather than mentioned in the fine print, which also might cause some confusion about profit from operational results versus results from the sale of real estate? And so on and so on.

According to Bear Stearns, which based its analysis on estimates that companies made in footnotes to their annual reports, if companies in the Standard & Poor's 500-stock index had counted options as a cost, their earnings per share would have been 20% lower in 2001 than they actually were.

On both sides of the Atlantic Ocean, too many boards have signed-off on reports that lack the necessary transparency to give a true insight into what is going on inside the company concerned. For 2001, the US Securities and Exchange Commission found fault with 350 annual reports from America's 500 biggest companies.[6] The major problem areas were:

- *Management discussion* – most companies fail to analyse industry trends, risks, cash flow and capital needs.
- *Accounting* – companies don't explain which accounting policies they use and how different interpretations of the rules would affect reported profits.
- *Revenues* – companies aren't telling investors what rules they use when deciding what to count as revenue, especially in technology, energy, pharmaceuticals and retail.
- *Impairments* – companies won't reveal how they adjust the figures when soft assets such as brands, patents and goodwill lose their value.
- *Pensions* – companies aren't always spelling out the interest rate and actuarial assumptions that they use to calculate liabilities on their pension funds.

The pressure for good bottom-line performance, high stock prices and bonuses being dependent solely on realizing quarterly or yearly profit targets has started to backfire. Enron went as far as placing assets offshore, off of its balance sheets, in order to show good returns on assets while hiding the risks connected with those assets. Royal Ahold's CEO was brought down by the revelation of an earnings overstatement of more than $900 million, due to overly aggressive recognition of vendor allowances in its US operations, a profit overstatement in South America.

These and other questionable practices took place after the Internet bubble, when shares were experiencing a serious bear market (a period when stock prices slide) and society was beginning to look more and more critically at the business world.

Share options themselves are also becoming worthless. In some countries tax authorities allow managers a limited rate of income tax on the value of their options (e.g. 7% in the Netherlands), if they pay the tax due at the moment the options are awarded. In some corporations managers are given company loans to pay these taxes. Shareholders, who may not be aware of these loans (which can amount to heavy obligations if the stock price stays below the awarded option price), can experience an unwelcome surprise the moment the loans become public. Similarly, several companies have had to supplement their pension obligations with additional contributions, partly because of the downturn in the stock market, but also because they have taken too many pension-contribution 'holidays'.

Cracks have begun to show in the financial sector. The viability of Internet-driven companies, the portfolio value of insurance companies, the degree of solvency in the economy, and the strength of the traditional management structure have all turned out to be less solid than assumed. The public at large has started questioning the integrity of business leaders.

Much has been written about why the system of accountancy checks and balances has not worked. The main issue is that stakeholders must be able to trust that the annual report is an accurate picture of a company's assets and liabilities. In many cases, the annual report is the only tangible representation of what a company is worth. The company's *value* can then be based on its past performance, its consistency in delivering sound returns on invested capital and its ability to continue delivering good results.

Making a judgement on *future* performance, however, depends on the reliability and soundness of the company's financial and intellectual capital. Transparency in such areas as execution capability and the company's competitive position will contribute to the possibility of evaluating future performance and to the safety of shareholders' investments. Accountants should realize that their signature on the accounts plays an important role in whether people's pension obligations and savings can be entrusted to a particular corporation.

As the annual report is *the* document on which outsiders have to rely, the issue arises of introducing new systems of checks and balances.

Cynicism among staff

It is not only in the financial arena that managers are feeling insecure. Even though highly performing staff are vital for corporate success, our experience is that a large percentage of well-educated middle managers aged between 25 and 35 will say that their potential is poorly used. Several reasons are given. They are allocated too many assignments that could be done, in large part, by people with less experience and education. In many cases, these tasks take up 75% of the average working day of the middle manager. Others claim that their bosses hold them back. They don't have the freedom to use their potential fully and contribute to the company in a way that could make a difference. The lack of knowledge-sharing at all levels in the organization is another common complaint.

But staff feel that the most irritating experience is when new senior managers come into the job (including CEOs) and take neither the time nor effort to find out what people know and might contribute to corporate performance. Too many senior managers arrive with a more-or-less fixed agenda and don't even start a dialogue about their staff's priorities or their assessment of the barriers to excellence. Too often, they hire outside consultants or listen only to their own viewpoint.

This tendency and the lack of structured top-down/bottom-up communication leads to a constant misalignment of the company's leadership agenda and of the operational agenda of the managers who are heavily involved in execution.

Talent losing ownership

During the 1990s, the 'talent issue' was high on everybody's agenda: 'The war for talent', 'talent is our most important asset' and 'a talent-driven organization' were phrases bandied about by academics as well as executives. The importance of talent – attracting it, developing it and retaining it – was never in doubt.

But some time during the last few years the feeling of 'ownership' among this talent has started to diminish. When this is added to the prevailing cynicism, talented people no longer feel like they are working for 'their' company. This has probably been caused by a shift in the way companies are operating as much as by the changing talent base.

Corporations have started to operate more and more like big governments. There are many rules and regulations. Management development programmes have become extremely formal, and training programmes are well defined and often spread over several years, with little room for individual adaptation. The size and structure of these big organizations has made it more difficult to challenge young incoming talent to the maximum, either emotionally (as people) or professionally.

People don't join a company to create shareholder value or meet next quarter's results – they want to have a great life, and their career is part of that. They want to be able to apply their knowledge, energy and creativity. They want to be fully stretched. The fact that companies are focusing on processes, efficiency, structure and digitization often doesn't help. Talented people long for the freedom and chance to prove themselves. They want their companies to be successful, make superior products and create excited customers. They want to boast to their friends and relatives about the great company they are working for. But all they hear is talk about creating shareholder value.

The talent base has also changed over the last few years. People are more individualistic and they tend to feel that the success of their own work is more important than the success of the company as a whole.

Power and authority drifting apart

The role of leaders has also subtly changed. The CEO and his leadership team are responsible for taking the company into the future and ensuring that the corporation keeps on outperforming its competitors in order to sustain a level of profitability that is better than its industry peers. Because of their formal position, they possess the power to lead their organization and direct their people in the way they feel is suitable.

Leadership is obviously more than mere power. Free, talented people follow their leaders not because of their hierarchical position, but because of the respect they have for them and their confidence in the leaders' integrity and the decisions they make. Authority has to be earned, and is given only when deserved. Good leaders create transparency, assign accountability, take responsibility, and in this way have both power and authority.

During the last few years, we have seen political leaders around the world who possess the formal power to lead their countries, but are separated from their citizens by a policy of short-term thinking, a focus on being re-elected and their political agenda. This agenda often differs from that of their fellow citizens. The latter's priorities (often safety, education, healthcare and employment) do not get sufficient attention or budget. This, added to an increasing amount of media coverage of corruption and scandals, has led to a growing lack of respect for politicians. As a consequence, some citizens feel justified in trying to avoid paying taxes and bending the law where possible.

In just the same way, corporate power and authority will slowly but surely begin to separate as corporations increase in size, bureaucracy enters deeper into organizations, talent starts to lose ownership and communication and clarity around decision making become more and more problematic. This is exacerbated as CEOs focus increasingly on the demands of Wall Street, the media begin to discuss excessive executive pay and both investors and employees start to doubt the level of competence in corporate governance.

A new approach

In summary, too much concentration on the share price and the financial results aspect of the sustainable profit equation often leads to a management approach in which a company is steered mostly by financial key performance indicators. The average CEO has become too distant from the process of executing strategy.

We need a new approach that involves key executives in the process of aligning strategy and execution.

Energizing people

One of the main tasks of an effective leadership team is creating energy. All entrepreneurs realize that the moment they are able to transfer their personal enthusiasm into their company and their people, the leadership game is 90% won.

This task is difficult enough in a small, entrepreneurial organization. The entrepreneur runs around the company, talking to as many people as he can during the week, and creates company outings, lunches and other kinds of events to keep the momentum going. Nevertheless, the moment the enterprise becomes a larger corporation, the $1 million question is how to keep alive that spirit and drive.

We need to create a management system that brings the CEO and the leadership team into the middle of the corporation. We need to find an approach by which the management board can have a real-time dialogue with the people who make the difference – an approach that involves, directs and motivates the hundreds or sometimes thousands of people who will take the company into the future. And we need an approach that accomplishes this in such a way that momentum is not lost, leadership retains respect, normal reporting lines are not jeopardized and focus is maintained.

Utilizing talent

The task of any leadership team is to utilize fully the resources that have been entrusted to them. This applies particularly to human resources, and not merely because those holding the company's intellectual capital have the ability to walk out of the door at any moment if they feel they are not getting the recognition they deserve.

You attract and retain the best people if you involve them, challenge them and stretch them to the utmost. We are all searching for a business concept that enables talent to excel, knowledge to be shared and best practices to be adopted.

Towards an aligned operating arena

Human beings need to feel included. Within this inclusion, psychological freedom is necessary for managers to create excellent products and services. But we also need a common corporate purpose, and boundaries so that we don't wander around blindly without focus. These boundaries are determined through the company's purpose, values, strategy and organizational capabilities.

In the next chapter, we will define the arena where all this takes place, and where strategy and execution are aligned: the *operating arena*.

Lessons learned

- A short-term, quarter-by-quarter orientation creates a culture attuned much more to the financial analysts than to key people within the organization.
- Simple explanations don't always exist. It has become increasingly difficult to reconstruct the causal chain behind many events because of the vast increase in interconnectivity and the exceptional amount of knowledge needed to track all phenomena.
- Power and authority have a tendency to drift apart if the leadership lacks the willingness to involve key people in crucial issues of strategic alignment.

3

The Operating Arena: Aligning the Space

The operating arena is a central concept in *management beyond control*, our approach to aligning strategy and execution to address the challenges of managing the twenty-first-century organization. This chapter will explain what an operating arena is and how a company can shape this arena in its own unique way, using the best organizational capabilities to execute its strategy.

Alignment can only take place if there are measurable parameters. The operating arena is defined by 39 measurable categories of capabilities chosen as the result of extensive research. In this chapter, we give some examples of how these capabilities are related to the execution of strategy and why they are instrumental in the alignment process.

The operating arena explained

What is an arena? A place where action happens. The Romans had their gladiatorial combat, a circus offers its entertainment, theatres have their performances and corporations conduct their operations in arenas.

Imagine the CEO of a large multinational corporation visualizing his worldwide working space. What does he think of?

All over the world, there are managers of different races and different genders, senior people as well as young, eager talent just out of university. At project team meetings budgets are drawn up, failures reprimanded and successes celebrated. Factories are operating at high speed, producing products with often the right, but sometimes the wrong, customer appeal. There are offices in different places, and both old and new facilities. The CEO searches for the best practices for his teams and visualizes how managers might recruit the best talent, although he also knows there are good people leaving the company. He thinks of press clippings in different languages, and of images being created and values strengthened as well as destroyed. He sees bosses who lead with an iron fist as well as managers who favour a participative management style. He knows that some of his people are negotiating with unions, others with local governments or pressure groups. Salespeople are meeting with buyers, IT structures are being refined and market research is continually taking place. He experiences excitement as well as responsibility. He also experiences the distance.

This is his working space, his theatre of operations. The sum of all the attributes that make up the enterprise constitutes his operating arena.

Most CEOs have come up through the ranks before reaching their top positions. They used to be in the middle of the arena. What happened?

When Fred joined the board of ASKO AG, Helmut Wagner, his German chairman, took him into his office and said, 'Fred, hier im Vorstand kann man nichts bewegen' – now that you are a member of our executive board, stay out of the action and leave the operational activities to the divisions.

His reasoning was clear. The company had competent executives leading the different divisions. My responsibilities were corporate. As a result, what was happening deep in operations was black boxed for me.

We know how risky this is. We have to get the CEO *back* into the middle of the company. And we have to do this in a way that leaves the arena intact and lets the 'right' reporting lines retain their function.

A dynamic space

The best guarantee of success in business today is to create a culture of respect as well as an innovative environment in which people want to advance but also expect to be led. The kind of company we are advocating is run with a system that offers freedom for talented individuals, but also boundaries within which they can work. The boundaries reflect the organization's sense of purpose, the definition of its intent and its culture.

This intent is designed to clarify what the company stands for, what its leadership really wants and does not want. Past experience shows that communicating a credo or publishing a mission statement in the annual report or on the corporate website is not a sufficient guarantee of focus and clarity, nor is producing strategy papers or maintaining a perfect budget and target structure. The challenge lies in creating a *working environment* in which the company's ambition is clear, the strategy is understood and accepted, accountability is given and taken, initiative is stimulated and people are positioned so that they can be responsive and resourceful.

The *operating arena* is the quintessential interface between strategy and execution and should be custom-designed and custom-managed. It is not merely a set of objectives, nor is it the vision or the strategy – it is a set of organizational capabilities (Figure 3.1).

Therefore, successful CEOs should be concerned about, and actively involved in, managing their operating arena. This is the space where the action takes place and where they can now digitally walk around, convening and communicating with their most talented executives on a regular basis. Actively managing the operating arena requires a different management approach.

Figure 3.1 The operating arena

The principles of this approach – managing by strategic pull and operational push – are built on four fundamentals (see Chapter 7). Embracing these fundamentals provides a degree of comfort that even a large corporation can be governed, guided and controlled. Measurable systems can be established within which people can excel and achieve sustainable competitive advantage and profitability for their organization. It is like 'fencing in' the theatre of operations – it gives you freedom within borders. The organization concentrates on *what to achieve* and *what to align*.

If the operating arena is designed and managed well, CEOs can expect their company as a whole to be more intelligent, more agile and more creative. Complexity can be handled, freedom can be given and transparency and accountability can be enforced, while people also deal with risk and thrive on uncertainty. The philosophy behind managing an operating arena is to let the corporate dialogue do its work, drawing on the organizational intelligence and allowing people to solve their problems in the most suitable way. Compared to managing by outcome objectives alone, managing the operating arena requires that leaders assume responsibility for convincing all managers that openness, letting go, and dialogue really work, so they actively start managing the company from the middle. The challenge, of course, is to allow existing reporting lines to keep functioning and find the right inspirational touch that keeps people realistic.

We define the operating arena as follows:

An operating arena is a dynamic space, a portfolio of organizational capabilities, designed to maximize the alignment between strategy and execution.

If the operating arena is clearly described and understood, CEOs are able to measure and manage those formerly 'immeasurable' organizational capabilities that eventually determine the achievement of objectives.

Managing the operating arena is a continuous process that assesses corporate capabilities and compares them to the intended strategy and objectives. Thus, this assessment is not solely focused on performance, nor is it a one-time event. It permanently aligns organizational capabilities and resources with the projected goals. The operating arena is the place where one continuously strives to align the organizational agenda with the strategic agenda, and vice versa. It enables companies to deal with emerging challenges in real time, because there is no delay in feedback about performance. There is no need to wait for results coming out of the standard reporting systems. That is why this permanent process of alignment between strategy and capability makes companies more agile, more innovative and more manageable without the need for burdensome control mechanisms.

The strategic alignment agenda

The alignment agenda is the principal guideline for managing strategic alignment. It emerges from the alignment between the strategic agenda and the organizational agenda (Figure 3.2). Setting and managing this alignment agenda is a joint effort between the CEO and the leadership team on the one hand and key executives on the other. (We will discuss participation and agenda-setting later in the book.)

Figure 3.2 The strategic alignment agenda

An effective alignment agenda addresses the most critical capability and organizational improvement issues that require continual attention and alignment. They are the issues that the CEO, the leadership team and key executives consider vital for corporate success in the short and medium term. They represent the company's *priorities*.

Therefore, control can evolve into guided interaction, which allows people to transform emerging and growing complexities into competitive advantage. In this way, managing the alignment agenda brings us to a level *beyond control*.

Intended and perceived strategy

Frequently, companies have two kinds of strategy. There is the *explicit* strategy, set and approved by the board, presented to shareholders and analysts and written up in official company publications: this is the *intended* strategy. Then there is the *implicit* strategy, as exists informally in the organization: this is the *perceived* strategy.

If we define strategy as where to go and how to get there, executives operating in the middle of the organization are kept busy every day doing their regular jobs as well as finding practical solutions to save costs and outperform the competition. This is done through certain processes and within a culture that has become embedded in the organization over many years. However, this implicit strategy might all be quite different from what is written up in the board's strategy paper or the company's credo.

Explicitly defining the strategic agenda involves strategic and organizational issues as seen from the perspective of the CEO and the board. If the company's key people are able to assess and measure its organizational capabilities, it is possible to derive the implicit strategy as perceived by the organization. Even better, any misalignment between the strategic agenda and the organizational agenda becomes obvious.

The organizational agenda is defined by the desired level of organizational capability and by the *gaps* that appear after executives have assessed the company's *current* capabilities, for example by completing an organizational capability scan (about which more later). Synchronizing the CEO's agenda with that of the talent deep within the organization not only results in the creation of a shared strategic alignment agenda, but also helps the explicit and implicit strategies to be merged over time. All this leads to an aligned operating arena.

The theory of strategic alignment

In order to match their execution with their strategy, companies should have the sufficient organizational capacity for alignment. The fundamental prerequisites for this capacity are transparency and accountability (discussed in Chapter 2), which enable companies to operate within an aligned operating arena. This then implies that all the organizational capabilities needed for flawless execution will be at the required specific levels of quality.

Companies are aligned when their crucial people – the corporate leaders, managers and specialists in charge who truly determine the company's success – decide that the quality of the corporate organizational capabilities meets their expectations and enables them to execute the strategy.

Therefore, in order to gain strategic alignment, the current status of the organizational capabilities must meet the expectations of those who set the strategy, as well as those who execute the strategy.

The particular quality of organizational capabilities is measured by having key people report on the current and desired status of those capabilities. Barriers to execution will be identified by gaps between the current and desired status.

A company will have a suitable capacity for strategic alignment if its strategic intent, objectives, interaction and supportiveness demonstrate appropriate levels of transparency and accountability. In that case the *alignment score*, which measures the capacity for alignment, will be positive.

Aligning strategy and execution

Alignment requires leaders, executives and operating managers to confirm that the current perceived levels of organizational capability match the desired levels. Strategic alignment needs to be assessed by CEOs as well as the company's key personnel. However, to measure strategic alignment properly, the company leadership and key people need to provide their responses separately.

The CEO is ultimately responsible for the company's strategy. He will determine the strategic agenda and decide on priorities and timelines, based on the company's ambition and required targets, thus setting the intended (explicit) strategy. Consequently, the CEO will do his own first assessment of the *required* quality of organizational capabilities.

The company's key people execute that strategy. They decide on the required quality level for the capabilities based on their *perceived understanding* of the strategy. This may well be quite different from what the company's leadership has in mind.

In order to get alignment between strategy and execution, the desired capability scores need to be aligned. First, there is the leadership's view, based on the intended strategy. Second, there is the view of the company's key people based on their perceived strategy. This reveals their assessment of desired organizational capabilities and indicates their ambition. The two may think quite differently about the desired (needed) levels of capabilities.

Therefore, there are at least *two main causes* of misalignment: the difference between the perceived and the intended strategy (desired capability scores of the leadership versus the desired capability scores of the operating managers), and gaps resulting from current scores being lower than desired scores.

Measuring alignment of capabilities

The theory of strategic alignment defines two types of measurement:

- measuring organizational capabilities, based on the perceived strategy;
- measuring organizational capabilities, based on the intended strategy.

Measuring organizational capabilities, based on the perceived strategy

The organizational capability scan is presented to the company's key personnel and they are asked to assess the operating arena, as they perceive it. They then complete the survey on the status of the organizational capabilities, as they would like them to be, as well as how they assess the current status. With its perceived strategy (their reality) in mind, they assess the company's desired and current capabilities. (See the ABN AMRO example in Appendix III.)

Managing organizational capabilities, based on the intended strategy

The capability to execute strategy is dependent on an aligned operating arena. The gaps between the current and desired status of the company's organizational capabilities need to be closed. The desired status should be based on the intended strategy – that is, what the company stands for, its ambition and its priorities. Therefore, any discrepancies between the desired scores formulated by the leadership and the desired scores given by the company's key people need to be addressed.

The analytical model

This measurement model emerged after several years of applying and developing our thinking at many corporations worldwide. The analytical model was originally based on 186 key organizational attributes, grouped into 39 categories, and covers a spectrum of seven organizational dimensions called sections (Figure 3.3). Together these form the portfolio of organizational capabilities that make up the operating arena.

The organizational capability scan

In order to find out what determines alignment, we began by considering the elements determining good execution. We looked at this from two angles: the viewpoint of managers actively involved in execution and that of professionals in the field of strategy. From these perspectives, we derived the large number of attributes that make up the operating arena.

Design

The operating arena can be considered as a set of organizational capabilities. This set (or portfolio) is the sum of all the relevant attributes, covering a wide range of organizational aspects. To give an idea of the type of attributes that have emerged, 10 very different examples from the total of 186 are listed below:

My company has
- The possibility of mobilizing resources.
- The capacity to provide knowledge and experience to employees.

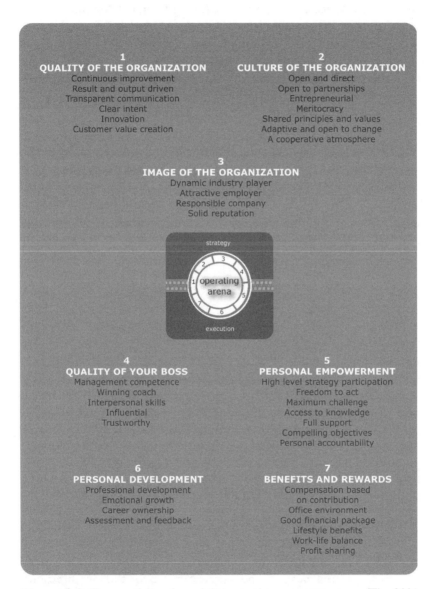

Figure 3.3 The portfolio of capabilities in the operating arena. (The 2006 mode update re-worded some capabilities, removed "Office environment" and brought back the "Re-invent for change" capability

- The existence of a strategy that is specific and understood.
- Fostering honesty and direct behaviour.
- A focus on meeting customers' expectations.
- Frequent assessment of people's activities.
- The possibility of leveraging managers' potential to the highest degree.
- Being a responsible member of the community.
- Openness to new ideas.
- Managing according to measurable KPIs (key performance indicators).

We performed factor analysis to group the 186 into 39 categories. These 39 categories, further grouped into seven sections, form an operational, measurable model.

Measurement method

Managing alignment means managing these clusters of attributes forming the organizational capabilities. It involves accountability, which requires measurable yardsticks. The measurement of organizational capability through the assessment of a company's key personnel – those who have organizational and/or knowledge power – is based on the concept that their perceptions, if measured anonymously and correctly, can be considered to be 'hard data'. To manage by yardsticks, most of which are considered to be 'soft', requires a measuring instrument with which both operating managers and all other company stakeholders feel comfortable. For such an instrument to be effective implies several requirements:

- All attributes that make up a company's organizational capabilities and operating arena should be covered.
- A high percentage of the company's key managers who are asked to assess the desired and current status of the organizational capabilities should respond. A high response rate is also required over time.
- The assessment must guarantee anonymity.

- Not only must managers from different backgrounds and cultures understand the set of capabilities, but the model must also allow functional or cultural differences to appear.
- Assessing capabilities, especially those desired, should require individuals to reflect thoroughly on both the upside and the downside of the scenario. (Otherwise, people have a tendency only to consider the advantages.)
- The assessment should take as little time as possible.

These requirements have been brought together in an organizational capability scan called the MeyerMonitor:

- The 186 key organizational attributes, grouped into 39 categories, covering seven sections, comprise the full operating arena.
- The use of an Internet survey (in fact, a process of dialogue), and the fact that in most companies the CEO himself invites his key personnel to assess the company's ability to execute its strategy, has led to response rates varying from 70 to 90%. Direct feedback – participants can instantly compare their scores in all sections to the corporate benchmark – also supports the attainment of high response rates.
- There is a guarantee of anonymity and that individual results cannot be linked to an individual's name or email address. A 'Chinese wall' is created by passwords and through the use of a trusted third party.
- The survey is in many different languages, and there is also a glossary of what may be unfamiliar terms.
- The 'desired' scores provide a context for analysing the 'actual' scores and detecting cultural or functional differences.
- In order for people to score realistically their ambitions concerning the organizational capabilities, mini-cases appear on the participant's computer screen giving both the upside and downside of each capability, supported by the underlying attributes.
- Digitization has led to an organizational capability scan being accepted as valid by many companies and thousands of participating managers.

A company's business model or design should obviously be based on efficiency and effectiveness, while fulfilling customers' priorities and using the company's resources to the maximum. It should also be based on how key people in the organization *feel* it should function in order to make it possible for them to be fully engaged and do their job well. The challenge is to create an aligned operating arena in which managers have learned to *notice* certain things. The organization needs to learn how, when and where to be alert. With the strategic alignment agenda as its backbone, the whole company should be on the alert for opportunities for success and improvement.

To develop and apply our theory, we have relied on a multilingual, anonymous reporting platform that focuses on knowledge workers. This platform has been in use since 1999 at several large corporations as well as in public-sector organizations. Furthermore, some well-known business schools have employed it as a tool to help graduating MBA students reflect on the kind of organization that best fits their personal management profile.

Scoring methodology: The gap analysis

In most cases, participants are invited by their CEO to be involved in assessing their company's organizational capability. By giving the 'brutal facts' they not only communicate the barriers to sound execution, but also help prioritize the organizational challenges. They are asked a series of questions in each of the seven sections and instructed to indicate where they think the company actually is (current) and where they would like it to be (desired), as shown in Figure 3.4.

As we have seen, in order to assess alignment, measurement should not deal with absolute outcomes, but should compare the desired level (key people's ambition for the company) with the current level (the company's actual performance). This leads to the identification of gaps. The strength of 'managing by gaps' lies in the fact that it quantifies – and is able to address – the opinion of managers operating deep within the company. A high gap index can be the result of a high ambition level or a low current assessment (or both).

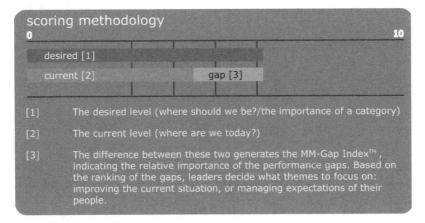

Figure 3.4 Scoring methodology for the organizational capability scan (See also Appendix I)

Therefore, a large gap can mean two things: either the current performance level is too low and/or the ambition level of the key people is too high.

Alignment and misalignment at work

Intended and perceived strategy alignment

Ambition levels can be managed both upwards and downwards. Imagine the following example. Managers have been complaining: 'This company is continuously pushing for better performance, we never get time to breathe'. Consequently, for the category 'Result and Output Driven' in the organizational capability scan, they score a desired level of only a 6. In order to execute the strategy in the highly competitive environment in which the company operates, this score is not acceptable. The leadership expects a desired score of an 8 or 9 for this category. This misalignment between the wishes of key personnel and the vision of the company's leadership needs to be managed carefully.

Here is another example: based on its strategic agenda, a company wants to strengthen the creation of customer value. The leadership of the company examines the outcome of the organizational capability scan for a specific division in a faraway country where the firm has a subsidiary. The results show no gaps in customer value creation: a current level of 6.5 and an ambition level of also 6.5. However, the leadership concludes that in this specific operating company the managers' desired ambition level on customer value creation is much too low. This needs to be managed upwards if the company is ever going to be a great creator of customer value.

These two examples show that sometimes the leadership has to decide to *not accept* the ambition levels shown by key executives – and, indeed, to seek purposefully to change them in order to align strategy and execution in the long term.

Aligning organizational capabilities

In order to align strategy and execution, the company's desired and current organizational capabilities should match. If not, the results of the capability scan will show gaps that need to be closed (see Appendix I). In Appendix V, we illustrate how over a period of three years Sara Lee/DE's management has worked on closing gaps.

Most companies that apply the concept of alignment follow a more-or-less identical procedure. It starts by the CEO inviting key people to get involved (for an example see Appendix II), followed by email messages that provide access to the organizational capability scan. Usually, a few weeks after the survey, the company provides specific digital feedback to the participants. In most cases this feedback includes a summary of the results, the management board's conclusions and priorities, and often the announcement that another scan will be conducted at some point in the near future.

A side effect

When a CEO involves his leadership team and key personnel in the assessment of organizational capabilities and the ideal operating arena, he creates feelings of involvement and respect. However, this only applies as long as action is being taken and accountability assigned. Misalignment will be instantly apparent when the outcomes of the separate scans, of both key people and individual members of the management board, reveal the ambition levels, the current status and gaps. These results will indicate barriers to execution that demand attention from managers at the centre of the company. The outcomes may also reveal certain internal (mis)alignment issues that specifically concern the leadership team. Note that, as distinct from all other participants whose answers are anonymous, scan results given by leadership team members can be identified back to the particular respondent.

Benchmarking

The availability of hard data about the corporate and divisional operating arena gives the company the ability to benchmark (Figure 3.5). It can benchmark itself against industry peers and benchmark different divisions against each other over time, or against a 'best in class'.

Benchmarking enables managers to assess the current position, and also to track how the company's organizational capability is strengthened or weakened over time. Similarly, individual parts of the operating arena can be clustered, visualized and benchmarked over time. In Chapter 10, the entrepreneurial aspects of SaraLee/DE's operating arena are discussed and these provide an illustration of how such clustering takes place.

'Hard' data about the level of alignment and the quality of the company's organizational capability are important, as we discussed above. The availability of a database against which to benchmark is also of great importance. No company is fully aligned and every company is confronted with capabilities that, according to its key people, can be improved. Therefore, it is vital to keep analysing over time and continually compare the organization with industry peers and best-in-class companies.

A management style for strategic alignment

We can only expect objectives to be supported, and thereby potent, if the strategy is clear and understood and there is effective interaction.

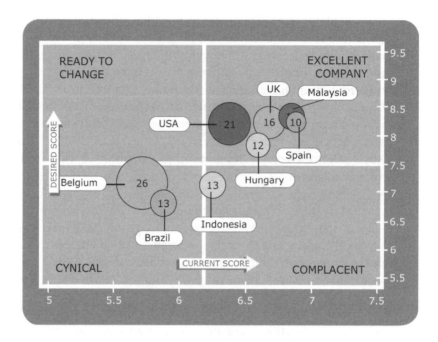

Figure 3.5 Benchmarking organizational capabilities. (The size of the bubbles is determined by the gap; the horizontal position determines the current level; the vertical position represents the ambition level.) Companies aspire to reach the northeast corner, with a small bubble.

Only then can we expect to have an effective, supportive organization. Also, we can only make managers accountable if the objectives and the level of supportiveness of the organization are measurable.

We need to specify in greater detail a management style that supports an effective corporate dialogue as well as a measurable framework to improve our company's capacity for alignment. Therefore, in the next chapter, we explain the principle of managing by strategic pull and operational push.

Lessons learned

- With current technology, CEOs are able to define and manage the notional space where all the organization's interaction takes place; what we call the operating arena.
- This operating arena is a dynamic space, composed of a portfolio of organizational capabilities where alignment between strategy and execution can be accomplished.
- There is a measurable and actionable definition of what this strategic alignment encompasses: companies are aligned when their key people conclude that the quality of organizational capabilities meets their expectations and enables them to execute the strategy. Key personnel are defined here as corporate leaders, the managers and specialists in charge: those who truly determine the company's success. Normally they are the CEO and his leadership team, together with key specialists and managers.
- There are various forms of strategic misalignment. First, there may be a discrepancy between the strategy intended by the leadership and that perceived by key executives. The second possible discrepancy concerns ambition levels. Key company executives may have aspirations above or below the levels required to execute the strategy.
- The strategic alignment agenda is the guideline for managing alignment between strategy and execution. It is the result of matching what the CEO wants with what those in the organization desire or think.

4

Leadership Beyond Control: Creating the Push

Managing by objectives is about defining, communicating and achieving goals. In contrast, our approach of *managing beyond control* incorporates strategic alignment, which refers to leadership that participates in operations to achieve those goals. In this chapter, we examine this approach, which we define as managing by (strategic) pull and (operational) push.

Creating a constant operational push is the ultimate proof of successfully managing beyond control. This requires leaders who aim to lead the organization 'from the middle'.

A company can only have a real capacity to be aligned if the strategic intent is clear, objectives are potent, interaction is effective and the organization gives its executives full support. Therefore, we introduce a model to define an organization that has an ideal capacity for alignment: we will call such an organization 'TransCountable'™ (transparent and accountable).

The ideal leadership

What does the ideal CEO look like? Jerry Useem analysed 100 years of CEO evolution, from a 'tyrant' like NCR's John Petterson to the 'administrator' and 'faceless' CEO such as GM's Alfred Sloan.[1] ITT's Harold Geneen was an example of the 'number machine', followed by a generation of 'statesmen' such as DuPont's Irving Shapiro and Chase Manhattan's David Rockefeller.

Useem called John F. Welch 'Neutron Jack' because of the way he assumed command of GE in 1981. Getting rid of whole layers of management and toughly addressing underperforming business units, he was a prominent example of a new generation of managers. During his 20-year reign, GE experienced a share-price increase of more than 5000%. As Useem observed, Welch and fellow CEOs of his type shook up corporations before anyone demanded it, and before the corporate raiders came on the scene.

Lee Iacocca, Ford and later Chrysler CEO, exemplified the 'celebrity' CEO. This type of leader confidently presented himself on television and at numerous press conferences. Then people like Sunbeam's Al Dunlap appeared, who cut costs mercilessly and turned out to be an eventual 'destroyer' of shareholder value.

At the end of this century of all kinds of different CEOs, it seems that we are once again entering a period of change. The *TransCountable* CEO has emerged: determined, balancing future performance with today's bottom line, a little humble, realistic and open. Daniel Vasella, CEO of the Swiss pharmaceutical giant Novartis, describes this kind of CEO's preoccupations as:

Failure. It is the prospect of failure, of course, that keeps CEOs up at night. But I would argue that there is another, less talked-about risk that may be more treacherous in the end. That is success. Or rather short-term success – what chief executives and Wall Street analysts call 'making the quarter.' . . .

From the beginning you must ask yourself one question again and again and again: What really matters? Which actions are really fundamentally important for the success of this company and its constituencies (namely shareholders, customers, employees, and the community at large)? . . . If you do your job as CEO and strive for what really matters, your shareholders will benefit over the long term.

It is not enough to be truthful to you only. To me transparency means that I will communicate truthfully what I do and don't know about my company's performance and prospects, the doubts that I have, and the things that I don't doubt. . . . That's not to say one has to be naive and publicly share information that will harm your company from a competitive standpoint. . . . It may sound trite, but I truly believe my ability to keep shareholders' faith in our company depends in the end not on whether I make the quarter but on who I am, what my guiding principles in life are, my behaviour. . . . And this relates not just to the CEO but to the entire leadership team and the company culture it establishes.[2]

We quote Vasella at length not merely for his openness around the issues of transparency and accountability, but also for his behaviour representing his entire leadership team and the company culture it encompasses. Vasella, like other CEOs described in this book, might help form the profile of a twenty-first-century CEO.

Like any other CEO, a TransCountable CEO is primarily responsible for setting the organization's vision and strategy, creating a culture of respect and guiding his corporation on its road towards superior returns on invested capital. Superior returns are the end result. Managing the alignment is the way to get there. Aligning means managing by pull and push. But where do you start?

First, you need a commitment to TransCountability: the commitment to create an effective organization based on transparency and accountability. It starts with a zero-based measurement. Where are you now, and what are the gaps between the desired level of alignment and today's situation? What is your timeline? We expect the CEO to take personal responsibility for monitoring and managing the closing of gaps based on targets agreed for the four factors determining the capacity for alignment: intent, objectives, resources and interaction (Figure 4.1).

Aligning strategy and execution

Creating sustainable shareholder value obviously depends on being in the 'right' industry, but it also requires the organization to operate with the best possible business model. The business model defines what the company will do and how it will do it:

Figure 4.1 The four factors

- *What* to do is concerned with strategy and strategic positioning, including which markets and customer groups to select.
- *How* to do it concerns execution and depends on the operating arena – the portfolio of organizational capabilities.

As we saw in Chapter 2, the business success of companies like Dell suggests that the 'best' business model creates the highest return on capital invested and underscores the argument that companies should compete with business models instead of merely with products and services. However, a business model has to be formed, adapted and managed. As a combination of people, culture, systems, structure and processes, it is dynamic. It is a living organism. So the winning company will be the one that not only has the best model, but is also able to maintain it over time and therefore organize it in such a way that it keeps on creating the best products and services time after time.

If you were to ask them, many managers would confirm that although strategy formulation is important, the barrier to success can lie in its *execution*. This makes it even more odd that leaders have moved away from managing organizational capability and therefore from keeping track of the company's ability to execute its strategy. Why has the system failed in this way?

First, organizational capability has been difficult to measure, and therefore difficult to manage. Second, because they have concentrated on objectives that are related to outcomes (money, market share, customer appreciation and costs), CEOs have been afraid of interfering in regular reporting lines since that might blur accountability for those objectives.

Instead of the linear value chain of strategy formulation, execution and outcomes, we need to consider a holistic process of strategy formulation, organizational capability and execution. Strategy and execution can be seen as two ever-changing, dynamic gears that are continuously in motion. Organizational capability can be considered to be the wheel that 'keeps the show on the road'; a wheel that should continue rolling and whose capability to drive the company forward must be measured over time. This is an area from which the CEO cannot step away.

If CEOs are not to be afraid of speaking the language of execution as well as of objectives and results, there has to be a system that makes it possible to pay close attention to operational issues and organizational capabilities, without at the same time losing momentum or frustrating the efforts of the executives leading the divisions. More than ever, leadership involves *participation*. The challenge is to find a way of leveraging the CEO's time in order to achieve this participation.

Participation: Leading from the middle

If time and culture allowed it, most CEOs would love to participate in the value-creation process in some way. Many would acknowledge that they miss the opportunity to 'get their hands dirty' and most realize that it is essential to be in contact with the company's clients on a regular basis. They understand that in order to be competitive in a dynamic world, there should be room for real-time adjustments during the delivery process. Therefore, they need to have a grasp of customers' priorities and try to be as close as possible to the organization's innovation and value-creation activity.

Operating knowledge and awareness of constraints in the company's organizational capabilities can be found deep within the organization. This is where the company's talented people are faced with the limits of its executional capability day in and day out. The challenge of our new system is to create an operating arena where the CEO can be placed at the middle of the company.

To contemporary leaders, formulating strategy and monitoring results are basic tasks that are important elements of top management responsibility. Leadership activity has to be evident 'in the middle', where most of the action takes place and the company's key personnel are operating. This is where the CEO can ascertain whether people understand and 'own' what the company stands for. It is the place to keep the execution of the corporate agenda alive. It is where the CEO's ideas can be challenged, and where authority can be earned. It is where priorities become manifest and inspiration is attained.

For their leadership to be meaningful, leaders need to both inspire and facilitate. They have to communicate a common cause and therefore provide a challenging perspective on the business. People need to be inspired in their daily tasks in order to achieve the targeted goals. The challenge is to develop engagement, obtain total clarity about what the company stands for, and create an atmosphere where managers not only look at their individual tasks but are also committed to the company's overall agenda. Inspiration and facilitation can be realized at arm's-length, but leadership from the middle is particularly about participation. Effective leaders are often known for the distinct ways in which they participate and communicate. Leadership by example, if done well, usually leaves a powerful mark on the organization. It is active behaviour that demands to be followed and not, for example, PowerPoint presentations. Physically (or today virtually) being in the middle is a good place to set the example.

Many people were surprised when Bill Gates stepped away from the CEO position and became chief technology officer of Microsoft. But, perhaps, he realized that 'the middle' was a better place from which to inspire and be close to where great, complex ideas are formed into powerful and innovative software. At Microsoft, leadership does not merely happen at the top. Maybe this quest to be at the middle was one of the first new attempts by the CEO of a large multinational enterprise to look for a *different* system of governing and operating.

Combining power and authority: Creating a culture of respect

In addition to participation, working for and ultimately leading a company that has a culture of respect should be the ultimate goal for every professional. Many people would invest in, buy from or partner with a corporation driven by such a culture. Ultimately, respect is gained through integrity and intelligence.

Integrity means that the company delivers what it promises: for example, what it promises its clients in terms of quality, delivery times and specifications. This applies to all stakeholders. In a company run with integrity, shareholders will not be promised more than the company can deliver, business partners know what to expect, and promises made to managers ('high potentials' and all) and employees will be kept. Integrity has to be deeply embedded in the company's DNA if a culture of respect is to be achieved.

Integrity goes hand-in-hand with *intelligence*. In this context, we define intelligence as the ability to grasp relationships, and as the everlasting search for new combinations: for example, individuals looking for better ways of designing and marketing products, sharing their knowledge, serving clients, and so on. Finding new combinations requires an open and intelligent mind. Intelligence does not only apply to individuals, but can be attributed to the company as a whole. A company should be looking for new combinations to serve markets, design business models or create organizational structures. New combinations are necessary to find concepts that help bigger organizations operate effectively and efficiently.

Strategy execution will be swift and determined if you are able to unlock the wisdom embedded inside the organization and combine and align this with the experience and intelligence of the leadership team. If a company is driven by intelligence and integrity, a culture of respect is the natural consequence. What is more, leadership will have both power and authority.

Unfortunately, as we discussed in Chapter 2, power and authority have drifted apart in too many organizations, often because leaders have disappeared from the middle of the organization. In order to understand why this is significant, we need to go a little deeper into some of the more fundamental principles underlying the operating arena and its management by pull and push.

Managing by strategic pull and operational push

The time has come to set the operating arena in motion. What does it take to focus the corporate dialogue on the right issues?

The traditional backbone of corporate control is the budgeting and targeting infrastructure. This, of course, is combined with regular formal and informal meetings between bosses and subordinates. The CEO and the leadership team set the strategic agenda, which serves as a directional input for the budgeting process. This entire sequence of activities is meant to define and shape the preferred commercial results, for the near- and long-term future. Here, the principal roles of the CEO are to oversee the process and whenever necessary to inspire and facilitate key personnel in the organization.

This sequence of strategic conceptualizing, agenda-setting and budgeting represents the *strategic pull* mechanism. It is about placing yardsticks somewhere out in the future, with several milestones positioned along the route, close enough to be seen yet far enough ahead to be challenging. Typically, this exemplifies the principle of managing by objectives, which aims to pull an organization into the future along a defined route.

Measuring and managing the operating arena adds operational push to the strategic pull. While managing by objectives puts a clear focus on what to achieve, managing beyond control incorporates those objectives but is also concerned with asking how the company's objectives can be achieved.

Management by objectives is about formulating and achieving goals (strategic pull).

Managing beyond control includes strategic alignment, which is formulation, facilitation and participation with regard to achieving goals (managing by pull and push).

The key word for managing by objectives is the *scorecard*. The key words for managing beyond control are *alignment, measurement* and *dialogue* – interaction about the score and about how to achieve that score. Continuous dialogue enables real-time alignment of strategy and execution. It allows for very precise and prompt operational or strategic adjustments, enabling quicker responses than most traditional budget or target feedback cycles. It creates better, shared agendas and, our experience shows, it prioritizes the often hundreds of projects that are running in most big corporations.

The operating arena should allow operational push initiatives that support the strategy taking place. Hence, it is important to note here that its purpose is not to formulate basic strategies. Strategy *formulation* should be kept at the top of the company. What the operating arena does do is enable strategy *formation* to be a combination of the formal process of strategy formulation and feedback coming out of the organization. This feedback is not only about the regular business process and results, but also about all the experiments and trials, and therefore about all the smaller and bigger failures that take place during implementation. Watching the strategic alignment agenda and monitoring the projects under this agenda give good insights into the strategy formation process.

There is one other advantage of being close to your key people in the operating arena. They also function as the company's conscience: they are *the* benchmark of how well the company is doing. They are much more critical of corporate performance than people outside, such as clients and analysts. So, if as a CEO you can meet the expectations of your talented people, the job will be all the more rewarding, because the company will continuously outperform the expectations of clients or any other outside stakeholders.

Managing is only possible if we can measure consistently over time. Since, as we saw in Chapter 3, the operating arena (the portfolio of organizational capabilities) is the vehicle through which the organization is able to fulfil its purpose, we need to define it as tightly as possible and be able to measure it. This is not an easy process; nevertheless, in order to be analysed the operating arena must be measured. Only then can we make a judgment about its capacity to align strategy and execution, and only then is it possible to manage the operating arena based on *hard* facts.

Measuring the capacity for alignment

In addition to conducting an organizational capability scan, it is essential to develop a score by which an organization can assess its capacity for alignment. Creating this capacity requires a certain mindset. There needs to be a willingness to involve key personnel in measuring the quality of the company's operating arena and to act on the outcomes. These elements demonstrate transparency and accountability: measuring and sharing data have immediate effects on transparency; acting on the data generates accountability. The right types of transparency and accountability lead to an optimal state of strategic alignment.

We want to emphasize that this *capacity for alignment score* does not say anything about the *quality* of a company's strategy. It is merely an indication of how well an organization will be able to execute the intended strategy, be it good or bad.

Transparency and accountability can also benefit outside stakeholders. Investors always look for indicators concerning a company's future performance, so creating transparency by publishing data in the annual report concerning the company's ability to execute may prove helpful. (There is more on this in Chapter 9.) Merely publishing the fact that a corporation enables its people to assess organizational capability on a regular basis should provide additional confidence for outside investors.

The measurement model

In the model for measuring the capacity for alignment, a fundamental division has to be made between strategy and execution. In the *strategic* domain, CEOs formulate the strategic directions and translate these into objectives. To achieve these objectives, however, the organization needs to be sufficiently aligned and capable. Alignment and capability are instrumental in defining the *execution* domain, which is where the available resources are located, communication takes place and operational decisions are made.

People prefer to operate freely in a transparent organization, though at the same time there is a need for clear guidelines and accountabilities. These are preconditions for all organizations; however, successful companies have often built a specific *system* with clear constraints and boundaries within which people can work. These boundaries are determined by the company's well-defined and understood strategic intent, and are within a framework or system in which people are given maximum freedom and responsibility to operate.

Formulating preconditions provides freedom within borders. Rather than telling people what to do and how to do it, you talk with them about alignment and what to achieve. Compared to managing by objectives alone, the difference here is that the company also quantifies the clarity of the strategy and the responsibility for the quality of interaction, and is able to assign quantified accountability for the availability of resources.

We call companies that operate in a transparent and accountable way TransCountable (see Figure 4.3 later). We have introduced this term mainly so we can describe the profile required to keep a company aligned. Our theory and methodology entail a pull and push management approach resulting in transparency and accountability: in TransCountability.

Four factors: intent – objectives – resources – interaction

An effective operating arena contains two domains – strategy and execution – which should both be transparent and accountable.

Which key factors typify an aligned operating arena? Within the given preconditions, four driving factors have emerged both from experience and statistical research. They are set out in Figure 4.1 and represent the building-blocks of the *capacity for alignment model*. We have learned that these factors reliably and consistently indicate a company's capacity for alignment.

Four questions

There are four questions linked to the four factors, which serve as the typical starting point for analysing a company's capacity for alignment (Figure 4.2). Each question identifies particular characteristics of an aligned organization, defined in terms of transparency and accountability.

Question 1: How clear is the intent?

A common cause unites people and gives a company its sense of purpose. Therefore any self-respecting corporation establishes its purpose or intent in one form or another. Intent is designed to create

Figure 4.2 The four questions

clarity about what a company, or a leader, really wants or does not want. Communicating a credo or publishing a mission statement has turned out to be insufficient to constitute a sound 'border' within which people can apply their freedom and creativity. In order to translate strategic intent into clearly formulated and shared objectives, it needs to be communicated, understood and 'owned' by all the company's stakeholders, and particularly by its key executives. If that is the case, the organization will be positively stretched by the absolute transparency of its intent.

Again, it is important to note that the score on this specific aspect does not judge the inherent quality of the strategy. Our focus is strictly on measuring the transparency of the corporate intent as perceived by the key people in the organization. The category and attributes determining the score behind this question are:

A4 – Clear intent
- Has a clear mission and strategy.
- Has a strategy, which is broadly known within the organization.
- Has a strategy whose specifics are understood.

Question 2: How potent are the objectives?

Objectives are not only a measurement tool for keeping score, but for focusing and energizing people. By 'potent' we mean objectives that are compelling, attainable, understood, measurable and rewarded. Managers should be able to relate them to their own objectives, so that these objectives can provide clear guidance to help people do their jobs.

Sometimes leaders formulate objectives without sufficiently taking into account how these goals will be perceived, lived by and shared; in other words, how they become an integrated part of the operating arena.

Our conclusion is that the strategic intent will not be effective if the related objectives are badly defined, because this means that accountability is weakened, results are not measurable and it is difficult to reward people commensurately. Therefore, we also often see a relationship between the size of the gaps related to objectives and those related to meritocracy.

CEOs who wish to operate with a culture of meritocracy should also want to cultivate people's accountability, and responsibility for this starts at the top of the organization. The categories and attributes determining the score behind this question are:

E6 – Compelling objectives
- Provides me with clearly defined objectives.
- Translates organizational goals into inspiring personal objectives.

E7 – Personal accountability
- Fosters an organizational discipline about attaining results.
- Holds me accountable for meeting my objectives.

Question 3: How supportive is the organization?

Optimizing the allocation and use of resources, both material and nonmaterial, is a typical managerial responsibility. It is essential that bosses manage and measure this aspect carefully. The managers' competencies combined with the environment in which they operate determine success. This environment should be supportive in all its aspects. People want material as well as emotional support; they want the freedom to act, as well as full support from their superiors. They expect the organization to create an environment without constraints, where they can learn, earn and contribute to the success of the company by fulfilling their potential.

Establishing accountability around this domain is a key ingredient in creating employee commitment and engagement. Being successful in this area is probably one of the strongest indicators of a well-managed business versus a mediocre one. The categories and attributes determining the score behind this question are:

E2 – Freedom to act
- Gives me control over my own activities and direction.
- Provides the freedom to make a decision independently.

E5 – Full support
- Gives me access to vital resources in order to perform my job.
- Gives me the possibility to mobilize resources.

Question 4: How effective is the interaction?

Interaction is not only vital in the creation of an effective operating arena, it is one of the four factors contributing to the capacity for alignment. Managing from the middle of the organization creates a requirement for dialogue and CEOs want to reach out so that they can share their ambitions with people at all levels. They want to communicate their agenda and find new ideas and solutions deep inside the organization. They want to listen, understand, challenge and be challenged – if only obstacles such as physical distance, the company hierarchy or their schedule would allow. If communication were perfect, decisions clear, projects clearly understood and reactions timely, organizations would function so much more effectively. Data from organizational capability scans show that in all organizations, private as well as public, dialogue is the biggest challenge. First, though, CEOs need to accept that their authority is not given by right but has to be earned. A culture of mutual respect needs to be created, freedom given, boundaries set and fear transformed into shared uncertainty. All of these elements are part of the creation of internal dialogue. The categories and attributes behind this question are:

A3 – Transparent communication and decision making
- Has effective dissemination of information.
- Has efficient internal communication.
- Has transparent decision making.

B1 – Open and direct
- Fosters honesty and direct behaviour.
- Expects people to give direct feedback.

The TransCountable company

No company will have a perfect, 100% capacity for alignment. Based on our research, experience and 'best-in-class' examples, we consider that companies showing a gap profile as in Figure 4.3 or lower can be

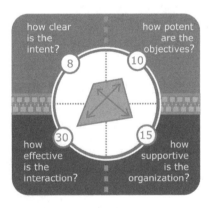

Figure 4.3 The TransCountable company

considered to have a good capacity for alignment. These are TransCountable companies.

Note that the minimum gap profile in Figure 4.3 still allows for gaps varying from 8 to 30, depending on the particular aspect of TransCountability. The reader is reminded that such gaps – a quantification of the differences between 'desired' and 'current' scores from the organizational scan – still need to be monitored even when they seem to be low and therefore safe. Even when a company fulfils these statistical conditions and can be considered TransCountable, any movement, especially in the desired/ambition levels, will remain of vital interest.

Benchmarking the capacity for alignment

Benchmarking can be done internally as well as externally. Some companies we have worked with use the *capacity for alignment index* to compare divisions or large business units against each other. These data help the leadership team to pinpoint areas of challenge, and form an excellent basis for having 'capability discussions' between the management board and a divisional or business-unit chief. But it also might be beneficial for the organization to benchmark its capacity for

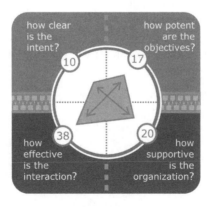

Figure 4.4 The capacity for alignment score (global benchmark)

alignment against the current industry benchmark, and/or the global benchmark (the latter is shown in Figure 4.4). This global benchmark indicates that interaction is the greatest challenge (gap index 38) for most companies, followed by facilitating a solid resource context (gap index 20).

Lessons learned

- Twenty-first-century leadership seeks effective ways to manage from the middle of the organization.
- Talented people like to be led from the middle and want to take responsibility for participating in the creation of the company's strategic alignment agenda.
- Management by objectives is about formulating and achieving goals (strategic pull).
- Management beyond control includes strategic alignment, which incorporates formulating, facilitating and participating in achieving goals (managing by pull and push).
- A minimum level of capacity for alignment is required to start the alignment process successfully.
- There are four questions linked with determining the capacity for alignment: (1) How clear is the intent? (2) How potent are the objectives? (3) How supportive is the organization? (4) How effective is the interaction?
- Companies with a high degree of transparency and accountability will possess the capacity for strategic alignment. We call these firms 'TransCountable'.

Part II

Creating Alignment:
The Continuous Dialogue

In Part I, we built a foundation for the introduction of a new concept for the leading of large companies. We defined the operating arena and presented a new mindset, namely a new approach of management beyond control.

In Part II, we will discuss the process of implementing *management beyond control* in the actual business environment, and the different tools available to achieve this aim. We address the follow question: What steps do we have to take to create strategic alignment?

5

The Corporate Dialogue:
Activating the Agenda

As we have seen, the strategic alignment agenda results from aligning the strategic agenda (formulated by the managing board) with the operational agenda, matching the strategic with the key operational priorities. This alignment process is a way of creating the strategic alignment agenda, but then the true challenge lies in keeping it alive throughout the organization, and maintaining the momentum is the subject of this chapter.

Measuring, matching and managing

The process of management beyond control is based on *corporate dialogue*, which involves measuring, matching and managing a company's strategic alignment (Figure 5.1).

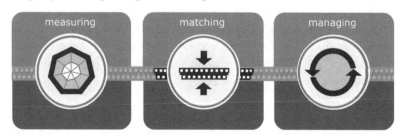

Figure 5.1 Measuring, matching and managing: three elements of pull and push management

Measuring the operating arena is the first step in this three-stage process towards the creation of an aligned organization. It is a well-known management dictum that you can't manage if you don't measure, but it is particularly true in the process of alignment. Measurement has to be a continuous activity, focusing not only on financial results, but also on the level of organizational effectiveness.

The second stage in the process, *matching*, is about creating the strategic alignment agenda by aligning the strategic and organizational agendas. The matching process generates an alignment agenda and a list of priorities and projects to maximize the alignment between strategy and execution.

As time goes by and situations evolve, the operating arena needs to be managed (stage 3), while the strategic alignment agenda needs to be periodically revised and kept alive. This *managing* activity should not be neglected or handled in an unstructured way. Management beyond control demands that the measurements of organizational capability are kept up-to-date, but in particular it means that the dialogue between the CEO and his key executives should be continual, highly structured, highly relevant and well-programmed. The management beyond control process serves as a real-time link between strategy and execution. It is about building the infrastructure necessary to create strategic alignment so a company's key personnel can be led at the required pace in the desired strategic direction. The *executive dialogue centre* (see Chapter 6) sits beside measuring and matching as the leadership support tool that makes it possible to reach out to people deep inside the organization.

Strategic alignment can be attained by maintaining a well-balanced attention to both capabilities and actual performance. What is required is the CEO's firm attention on financial results – to the 'finish line', so to speak – through the regular budgeting procedure, as well as a firm eye on capabilities via a process in which he communicates with a large group of managers, in effect leading from the middle.

Measuring, matching and managing are the three fundamental elements of the *management beyond control* leadership style. However, 'beyond control' does not mean being *out* of control. In fact, because his key talented executives are also involved, the CEO is more than ever beyond control, confidently in charge of the strategic decision-making process. They provide the control *outcomes* and have the opportunity to share relevant ideas and solutions with him. The fundamental difference in management here is that, thanks to the continuous dialogue on the strategic alignment agenda, executives are not merely pushing budgets and targets, but are also proactively involved in the strategic alignment process.

Measuring

Managing performance is about the financial results of *today*; managing strategic alignment is about strengthening the company's capabilities to bring about the financial results of *tomorrow*. Both serve as an analytical backbone creating sustained profitability, and both complementary types of data need to be interpreted and managed:

- Performance (results) data.
- Organizational capability data.

It is important to note that when creating the strategic alignment agenda, performance data do have a role as they are primarily used to *support* the organizational capability data. In other words, the strategic alignment agenda is not the vehicle to obtain detail on performance issues such as sales achieved. That is why performance data next to capability data might be applied and interpreted as 'informers', to indicate where an organization may need improvement. Any barriers to execution will be identified by gaps between the current and desired status. The organizational data should provide actual insights into dealing with the improvement areas. In the left part of Figure 5.2, we see an example of the results of the organizational capability scan. The company's key personnel have assessed seven sections consisting of 39 categories making up the operating arena.

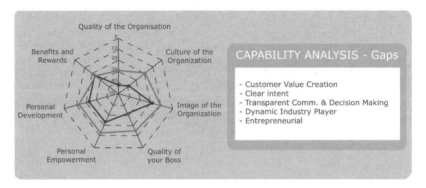

Figure 5.2 Measuring the alignment

Measuring the operating arena makes a company more alert and agile, because it focuses both leadership and operational attention on shaping the operating arena so as to guarantee future performance.

Knowing *what* to ask, *whom* to ask and *how* to ask are key elements in measuring organizational capability. The organizational capability scan introduced in Chapter 3 asks key executives to answer questions *anonymously*. The focus here is not on revealing individual opinions, but rather on identifying significant gaps between personal ambitions and perceptions of the organizational situation.

In order to learn more about the actual situation deep within the organization, you may want to ask people who are confronted with the effect of capabilities day in day out. Even then, some issues may need deeper analysis and more challenging questions. This is where dilemma questions come in.

The principle of a dilemma question is quite simple. Instead of asking about the current and desired state of affairs, it asks people to choose a direction between two distinct alternatives for change. For example, Figure 5.3 presents such an example about a company's capability to innovate. Here, the choice is between a structured culture on the one hand and a more entrepreneurial culture on the other. Results will indicate which statement optimally describes the current organization and which statement best describes where the organization needs to be. The outcome of this particular dilemma was

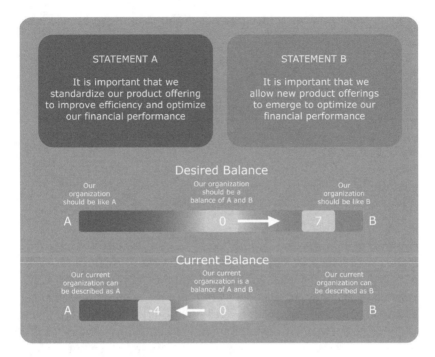

Figure 5.3 Example of a dilemma question

that although the company was currently strongly focused on standardization, the key people within the organization supported a shift to innovation. Through the organizational capability scanning process and various dilemma questions, we are able to gain an initial 'snapshot' of the current (perceived) state of the organization with regard to general or specific issues.

Ideally, this information serves to formulate an initial operational agenda. This agenda will represent an overview of common and specific organizational strengths and weaknesses at a particular moment in time. It is important to note, however, that initially the operational agenda is an *implicit* agenda, based on executing the perceived strategy. In the fictional example shown in Figure 5.2, based on the outcome of both the general capability scan (seven sections, 39 categories) as well as the dilemma questions, one can see that the organization is faced with five important 'gaps' to address, namely:

- Customer Value Creation
- Clear Intent
- Transparent Communication and Decision Making
- Dynamic Industry Player
- Entrepreneurial

Preparing for the strategic agenda

While the input for the operational agenda comes from executives, managers and knowledge experts inside the organization, the principal input for the strategic agenda comes from the CEO. Formulating a strategic agenda is often not as simple as it seems. For example, you may often want to limit the number of items it contains to six or seven, as each agenda item has to be linked to the capability scan data and may give rise to more than one improvement project.

Creating acceptance and (preferably) consensus on the strategic agenda among the company's leadership team is a starting point. The initial input is derived from strategy papers available in all large companies. The next step could be asking management board members individually to fill in the organizational capability scan. This may kick off interesting discussions. Depending on personal experience and preferences, different issues might be relevant to different members of the leadership team.

Creating the strategic agenda is often a CEO's first leadership challenge, including getting it accepted by his management board colleagues, despite the fact that ultimately it will probably be reformulated on the basis of the outcome of his key people's priorities. Particularly when we are dealing (as in most cases) with multidivisional and multi-country organizations, we have to distinguish between corporate data from the company as a whole and division- or country-specific data. This requires a sound analysis of the data from the capability scan.

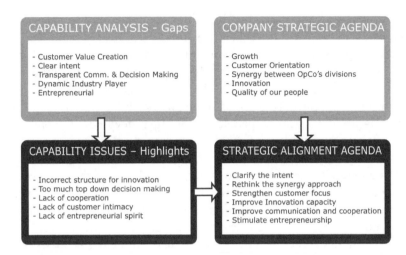

Figure 5.4 Matching the strategic agenda with the operational agenda

Matching: Creating the alignment agenda

The process of aligning the operational and strategic agenda to create the strategic alignment agenda can be very gratifying. We have seen firms taking different approaches, from half-day management board discussions on various priorities to digital broadcasts, together with other instances when capability data were extensively analysed by consultants and staff. Figure 5.4 explains the steps to be taken to arrive at an appropriate alignment agenda that focuses on the

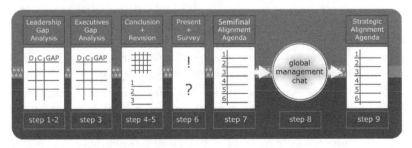

Figure 5.5 The formulation of the strategic alignment agenda

improvement of capabilities. Real-life examples of this alignment process can be found in Appendices III–V.

An appropriate strategic alignment agenda is the ultimate visible result of top company executives having captured the awareness of what is truly going on within their companies, and thus having captured that capacity to steer them in the desired direction. The agenda should energize people, keep them focused on company priorities, unlock their knowledge, provide an overview and make leadership visible. It should enhance stakeholder appreciation, strengthen competitive advantage and support corporate governance. This is why the matching process has to be taken very seriously. It is about leading from the middle, formulating, refining and embedding the strategy in the organization and the minds of its people. The better a strategy is aligned with current views and capabilities, the more successful will be its execution.

The alignment agenda consists *exclusively* of well-formulated, measurable capability targets. The gap results shown in Figure 5.5, resulting from the fictitious example of Figure 5.2, suggest the following capability issues:

- Incorrect structure for innovation
- Too much 'top-down' decision making
- Lack of cooperation
- Lack of customer intimacy
- Lack of entrepreneurial spirit

The CEO holds the final responsibility for the company's strategy, e.g. the choice of industry (where appropriate), its positioning in this industry and the business model to be followed. A chosen strategy then implies the setting of objectives, to be attained by means of strategic initiatives formulated by the Managing Board.

The formulation of the strategic alignment agenda then takes place in several steps, which allow for adjustment and involvement by key executives:

(See Figure 5.4 for a diagram of this formulation process and Figure 5.5 for how the following steps are related.)

- *Step 1.* The leadership team formulates its strategic initiatives and defines, in capability terms, the company's strategic agenda.
- *Step 2.* The leadership team fills in the organizational capability scan, which results in an assessment, from their strategic point of view, of the desired and current status of the company's organizational capabilities.
- *Step 3.* Key executives throughout the organization fill in the capability scan and assess the current and desired status of the company's capabilities. This process can be accompanied and/or followed by posing dilemma questions.
- *Step 4.* Based on the data analyses from the capability scan completed by the key executives, the leadership team does a reality check. Have the strategy and its objectives any chance of being successfully executed?
- *Step 5.* If necessary, the leadership team adjusts its strategy and objectives, and formulates capability improvement initiatives as a draft alignment agenda.
- *Step 6.* In electronic format, the leadership presents strategy, objectives and proposed capability improvement initiatives, accompanied by specific survey questions about possible barriers to realizing the proposed improvement initiatives. It is important to note here that, based on the quality of their responses to the survey in Step 3, key executives can effectively qualify and prioritize their participation in the 'management chat' described in Step 8. In practice, the key people selected for this will consist of 'emerging experts' in the subject matter and country/business representatives.
- *Step 7.* The leadership incorporates the outcomes of the survey in Step 6 in order to formulate a 'semi-final' strategic alignment agenda.
- *Step 8.* The CEO holds a 'management chat' with representative key personnel, to discuss the semi-final strategic alignment agenda and the capability objectives.
- *Step 9.* The ultimate strategic alignment agenda is complete – for that present time, of course, and only until it needs to be changed again.

The next step would be embedding the agenda into the full management process of the company. This means that the strategic capability alignment agenda and the strategic objectives are brought back into the profitability equation (sustained profit = financial results × strategic alignment) and made an integral part of the management procedure, so that both financial and capability targets are being pursued.

Managing

There is a considerable difference between providing sound strategic direction as a leader and *managing* that direction. In this respect, pull and push management is about showing, as well as managing, the way to go.

As well as just being common practice, obviously it is important for a leader to communicate his strategy and its respective objectives. But this is not enough, and leading reaches beyond giving direction and setting objectives. In the process of execution, people need to be supported with the right resources and the right information. CEOs who aim to lead from the middle of the company feel the responsibility to be personally involved in providing this organizational push.

The real challenge of providing organizational push as a CEO is to avoid becoming immersed in the details of day-to-day execution. The details are not what is important; rather, it is the conditions under which people have to do their work that need to be meticulously

Figure 5.6 Managing the alignment agenda

measured and managed. In other words, push and pull management is about dialogue; it is about managing the operating arena by:

- Aligning the strategic and operational agendas.
- Creating and communicating the alignment agenda.
- Keeping the alignment agenda alive (Figure 5.6).

Managers throughout the company appreciate organizational push. They realize that it means taking operational input very seriously together with any good, applicable ideas that will strengthen the company. It indicates that leadership is focused on meeting formulated objectives as well as providing executives with the necessary resources to meet them. In terms of organizational support, the CEO needs to know if people have the resources to do their work properly. This focus on organizational support is a sign of true leadership from the middle. A well-formulated strategic alignment agenda will make a tremendous difference in keeping the entire organization 'connected'.

Creating a shared, supported alignment agenda

Maximum clarity about the strategic agenda is important, although of course there are limits. It would be naive to disclose aspects of the agenda that, if made public, might endanger the company's competitiveness. Key executives want to be led with integrity, reliability and competence. This implies that they are willing to let CEOs lead as long as such authority has been earned. In Chapter 7, we will argue that in such a situation managers accept limitations on their freedom, including not being able to know everything. This means that they also accept that there are some strategic alignment agenda issues and information (for example, exiting a certain market or industry) whose distribution has to be limited to a small inner circle.

At the same time, if we want key executives to be engaged and alert for opportunities to improve the company's success, we need to make them partners in its path into the future and thus aware of the leadership's priorities. We want talented people to stretch their minds and embrace more than their day-to-day operational responsibilities. These people should have a larger personal agenda than simply carrying out their regular duties. Their agenda should include continually looking for good practices to be shared, as well as new opportunities to improve the company's performance. Top management needs to treat managers with respect and openness, not merely to encourage their personal engagement, but in particular to unlock all the wisdom and potential embedded within them.

Leadership style

Managing beyond control requires a certain leadership style. Unfortunately, not every CEO's personal make-up is fit for managing by strategic pull as well as by operational push. People's character, in combination with their upbringing and cognitive and social skills, determines who they are, which may then strongly influence their style of leadership. A thorough exploration of this subject might well require several books. Therefore, here are just some general thoughts about the style necessary to create a well-aligned company.

Really talented people don't need to be motivated; they motivate themselves. They only require the feeling that they are truly needed for the company's success. Those who are important in bringing the company into the future should be allowed to apply their potential to the full. Practising focus and direction on the one hand and openness to other solutions on the other hand requires *wisdom*. This is a combination of knowledge and experience, the latter being derived from success and failure, from years of trying, drawing conclusions and learning. Wisdom can be found inside the people and culture of the organization, but it should certainly be a feature of the CEO. He has the ability to construct new combinations from past experience, new knowledge and innovative ideas. Finally, he is the one who is primarily responsible for setting the 'right' strategic alignment agenda.

The CEO needs to have the ability to be a 'servant' leader, someone who wants to be repeatedly challenged, to explain over and over again, to defend, argue and if necessary backtrack on earlier convictions. On the other hand, he needs to know when to follow his own convictions, even when the majority of his executives think differently. But he also has to explain, many months later if necessary, why he decided to act as he did. He knows that people want to be led by someone who has respect for other people's convictions as long as they are shared with integrity.

The CEO can demand involvement. While talented people can always ask to be heard, rewarded and taken seriously, they also have the responsibility to contribute, otherwise they lose the right to speak. Creating a shared strategic alignment agenda demands that the CEO confront key personnel, time after time, about their responsibility and their duty to contribute. Management by pull and push is the backbone of the creation of a meritocratic culture, in which real talent can emerge and merit is rewarded.

The alignment agenda and cultural differences

Creating a shared alignment agenda in an extremely diversified, large corporation is not only a question of using dialogue to bridge different market situations and languages, it also implies acceptance of the different cultures represented by key personnel.

The sometimes considerable cultural differences between different nationalities within large companies have an influence on how the role of the individual is perceived in a team or hierarchy, and on what the agenda itself means. There are societies where people feel intensely responsible for their individual contribution, especially if they consider that this contribution will influence the decision-making process. Germany, Scandinavia, the Netherlands and the US are examples of this kind of society. In contrast, France, Spain and China, with their imperial or royal heritage, are strongly influenced by a centralized governance structure. In the past, the worst thing that could happen to a courtier was to fall out of favour with the king or emperor. As a result, it was important not only to flatter your superiors but also to consider your 'neighbour' as your enemy or rival. Therefore, communication in those societies was often somewhat insincere, if not duplicitous.

For these reasons, the direct approach of American, German or Dutch managers is frequently at odds with that of the French, Spanish or Chinese. For example, the French often don't seem to have an agenda, which can be a cause of grave irritation among the Americans and Germans. However, the French may perceive a well-defined agenda as pushy and believe that the other party is trying to force their will on them.

This kind of issue explains why managing large international corporations through pull and push management requires close attention to the tone of voice in the corporate dialogue.

Corporate storytelling

Everything happening around a company forms part of its 'story', and the corporate story is the root of any aligned company. Companies need to communicate their corporate story, and the CEO should be the chief storyteller. A good story is characterized by drama. It has a setting, a plot, specific characters, often starts with some kind of crisis and, it is hoped, has a satisfactory ending or resolution.

Take the Cisco story. A man and a woman (the characters) were studying and working at the Stanford University campus (the setting). Then something happened (the crisis). They were trying to pass information back and forth, but it turned out that the computer systems were not able to communicate with each other. These two people came up with a software solution that made it possible for these computers to communicate and Cisco was created (the resolution).

In our corporate story, the permanent 'crisis' is how to align strategy and execution, and our characters are the CEO, possibly his leadership team, and certainly the company's key personnel.

In this case, our story also needs a director. We suggest that the top executive in charge of communication can, and in many cases should, play this role. It is quite evident that the director and the leading character, namely the CEO, should form a closely integrated team, as they would when producing a good play or successful movie.

The distinctive nature of the corporate story should lie in the fact that, although there is a plot, the entire corporation (meaning the people within it) jointly adjusts the words, giving shape to the roles and the various acts and scenes. It is they who transform the story into a play and bring it to the stage.

The CEO needs to create a desire in people to be part of the corporate story, which is therefore about inspiration, recognition and keeping people accountable. It is about building and maintaining forceful strategic pull and operational push. It is also about confronting data about capability that may not always be welcome. It concerns the reporting on, and addressing of, accountability issues on corporate objectives, as well as providing sufficient resources to achieve them.

CEOs managing strategic alignment need to tell a story using a richer, deeper language than the normal elements of sales, margins, budgets, objectives and overheads. Integrating hard data and compelling stories brings the corporate dialogue to life.

As we have said, keeping the strategic alignment agenda alive is perhaps the most challenging task a leader may face. It is not quite the same as managing targets or budgets, but maintaining a structured ongoing dialogue around the full corporate story is a very rewarding responsibility. It is also crucial in getting and keeping the company aligned.

When the corporate conversation really starts humming, the need may arise for a more sophisticated infrastructure for communication. In order to transform a free-format conversation into a highly structured corporate dialogue, you may require a different mechanism for interaction that brings focus and consistency to the dialogue and energizes and stimulates the participants. This may be the right moment to establish an *executive dialogue centre*, and it is to this subject that we turn in the next chapter.

Lessons learned

- It is of key importance in management to maintain a strict distinction between performance objectives and capability objectives.

- Keeping a company permanently aligned requires a highly structured approach for measuring and managing organizational capabilities through corporate dialogue. This process involves three stages: (1) measuring, (2) matching and (3) managing.
- The measuring process takes place both at board and operational level. At board level, it determines the desired status of the organizational capabilities based on the intended strategy. At operational level, it is the desired and current status of the company's organizational capability that is measured, in light of the perceived strategy.
- The result of the organizational capability scan completed by the community of key people within the organization determines the operational agenda: i.e. what that organization wants. The strategic agenda, on the other hand, is determined from the management board's strategic initiatives and its assessment of desired scores for organizational capabilities: i.e. what the CEO wants.
- Matching the strategic agenda with the operational agenda produces the strategic alignment agenda.
- In order to execute this strategic alignment agenda, improvement projects have to be defined and accountabilities determined.
- Serious and structured efforts are required to keep the alignment agenda alive.
- Different nationalities have different attitudes towards the concept of agenda-setting. Leaders need to be aware of these differences.
- Creating a consistent corporate story should follow the same procedure as any good theatrical production: it needs a director, a storyteller, a plot, a setting, characters and a satisfying ending.

6

The Executive Dialogue Centre: Installing the Toolbox

As we have seen, management beyond control requires 'virtually' walking around, leading from the middle and managing by strategic pull and organizational push. A structured, institutionalized process and toolbox is required to create a shared strategic alignment agenda, prioritize improvement projects and regularly involve key personnel in the decision-making process. In this chapter, we illustrate what constitutes this toolbox – called the executive dialogue centre – and show how to create one.

The executive dialogue centre

The concept of the *executive dialogue centre* (EDC) has been specifically designed to manage the dialogue between the CEO and key executives and establish strategic alignment.

The EDC enables the CEO to move back to the middle of the operation and the company's key people to access virtually the CEO's office, sometimes invited, sometimes uninvited. In both cases, the aim is active participation in company policy-making. Essentially, the EDC is a leadership support tool for CEOs who want to involve their talent base and break through the barriers of bureaucracy. It assists leaders in directing and changing the company through pull and push management initiatives. The EDC is a virtual measurement and interaction space that is managed from the CEO's office.

In technical terms, the EDC is a web portal with limited and secure access. Although a comparison with the company intranet seems likely, the EDC is quite different. Most intranets contain general information about the company, ranging from press releases to sales results, and tend to be available to everyone within the organization. The EDC, however, is specifically designed for information exchange and interaction between the CEO and an exclusive group of selected key executives. It combines a browser-based interface and a managerial process to present facts and figures and manage dialogue around the different items on the strategic agenda (Figure 6.1).

Typically, the computer screen is divided up into three distinct areas: *Facts*, *Input* and *Interaction*. In the *Facts* area the relevant

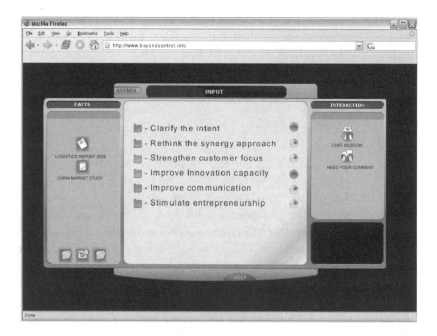

Figure 6.1 The Executive Dialogue Centre

reports, presentations and video footage related to the various strategic alignment agenda issues can be made available. It also contains the organizational capability measurement statistics, which are kept permanently up-to-date.

The *Input* area might display the strategic alignment agenda issues, thereby reinforcing its purpose as a guideline to keep the interaction focused on aligning strategy and execution. Or the *Input* area can serve as an interface for participants to complete surveys, answer (dilemma) questions and participate in real-time or off-line discussion forums.

The *Interaction* area provides an overview of the various dialogue aspects. Throughout the year, each agenda item will be the subject of a tailored structured dialogue between the CEO and a selection of key executives. These executives are selected either on the basis of knowledge, skills, experience, ideas or insights, or because their current positions enable them to contribute in some way. The EDC captures the outcome of the dialogue and ensures transparent feedback to the organization.

A structured dialogue is about setting objectives, sharing the underlying facts and organizational capability data, and structuring and moderating the interaction. This interaction can take a number of forms and is centred on true involvement and commitment: asking questions, making decisions, having discussions, introducing dilemmas, learning, educating, creating and innovating.

Who 'owns' the Executive Dialogue Centre?

Each of these forms of interaction has a time and a place. Sometimes there is no need or reason for questions or discussions. Sometimes, it is the time for instructions. This is why questions might arise about the ownership of the Executive Dialogue Centre (Figure 6.2).

Take the example of a management board of a large multinational enterprise. The board consists of five senior executives – the chairman and CEO, the CFO and three top executives – each responsible for a sizeable part of the corporation that is easily large enough to require a separate EDC.

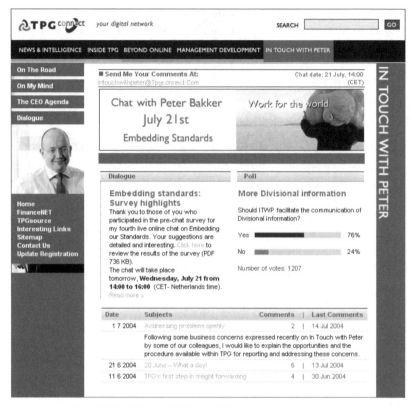

Figure 6.2 The Dialogue Centre owned by Peter Bakker, CEO of TPG

Every company can choose a different solution. In this case, each of the senior executives might create their own dialogue centre. Another company could create a separate virtual CEO office that only covers corporate issues. Other companies might integrate the two solutions.

With one click, a participating executive can enter the CEO's virtual office. There could be another button that gives access to the office (dialogue centre) of the board member responsible for a specific business. A password system can, of course, also guide access to the different centres.

Ten reasons for establishing an executive dialogue centre

1   It generates clarity about what the company stands for.
2   It facilitates the measuring, matching and managing process necessary to create strategic alignment.
3   It keeps the strategic alignment agenda alive.
4   It improves the quality of the company's decision making.
5   It prioritizes the different ongoing projects in the company.
6   It creates transparency and accountability for improvement projects.
7   It allows the sharing of knowledge throughout the company on subjects involving improvement projects.
8   It clarifies the responsibilities and accountabilities of individual board members concerning the strategic alignment agenda.
9   It personalizes the leadership.
10 It allows the board's 'excitement' to be shared with key people.

It generates clarity about what the company stands for

In an EDC, the CEO is able to share the company's intent, vision, mission and values using text, film, interviews or whatever else is necessary to create clarity. In this way, it can inspire managers in their daily tasks and create engagement. Furthermore, it makes it possible for people to look at their individual tasks and at the company's overall agenda. Most importantly, it allows 'defined freedom' for managers within which they are totally free to create and use their full potential to work for the company's success.

The CEO is able to listen to the different questions that his managers raise about the company's mission and strategy and the consequences these have for their day-to-day work. This kind of dialogue will help create clarity.

It facilitates the measuring, matching and managing process necessary to create strategic alignment

Managing alignment requires a conviction that openness, involvement, dialogue and measurement will produce results. It requires a systematic, structured, continuous and consistent process for inviting key personnel to give their assessment of the company's ability to operate effectively. The CEO should invite people to participate, and he should lead the process – and what better way than from his own virtual office?

The CEO's first challenge is to get a response rate as close to 100% as possible. How engaged is the talent base? Will they react immediately to the invitation? How many reminders need to be sent? The invited managers are asked, by email, to enter the EDC and give their evaluations within the 39 categories representing the company's operating arena. They score both the 'desired' and the 'current' states of the arena through the seven sections of the model. After they have completed all the categories, participants are immediately given feedback on their biggest gaps (between desired and current) and can see via benchmarks how they are doing in comparison to thousands of other managers, working for many other companies. This immediate 'reward' (seeing your scores benchmarked) starts the first thinking process.

Our experience is that companies invite participants to reassess the company about every 9 to 12 months. CEOs like to have a consistent measuring process in place over time.

The EDC can now be used for feedback. Participants are invited to come back and have a look at different scores. It is up to the company how much detail people are given. In most cases participants also find some kind of timeline for the next steps in measurement and agenda-setting.

Now the matching process begins. Will there be live meetings or workshops? How will the strategic alignment agenda be formed?

Basic input material can be found in the EDC's files concerning the company's strategic agenda and operational priorities emerging from the organizational capability scan. After a relatively short period, the result of the matching process should also be made available. A well-defined strategic alignment agenda has now been produced, and all key people have access to it. Now the managing process can start.

It keeps the strategic alignment agenda alive

The EDC can be very helpful in keeping a large enterprise's main priorities alive and visible. There are several ways to do this: for example, customers or any other stakeholders can be interviewed on film about a subject related to a specific capability challenge. Also, every two months, a special broadcast can be arranged on a specific agenda issue. Generally, it will start with the CEO explaining the issue. All over the world, participants can be online. Key people with a stake in the issue are able to participate no matter where they might be, and participants might be asked to react, hand in questions or make suggestions. In this way, facts concerning improvement projects relating to agenda issues can be registered, updated and made visible, which will certainly help in keeping the agenda alive.

It improves the quality of the company's decision making

The strength of the strategic dialogue and the possibility of inviting a worldwide talent base to enter the boardroom in order to make better decisions, and obtain support for the decisions being made, are best illustrated with a scenario.

The management board is meeting a week from today to discuss new responsibilities for the company's internal auditors. Specialists have prepared a ten-page memorandum and a specific one-page proposal. Accepting the proposal will probably improve the auditing process, but will have an impact on the way several hundred department heads work in the future.

Why not invite these managers into the EDC? Have them read the memorandum online, and let them make suggestions. You could even let them vote on the issue. All this has to take place before the meeting.

By following this approach, the management board meeting will now have input from all the managers who will be affected by the new internal auditing procedure. The following day people will be able to find the board's decision announced in the EDC. The decision will be accompanied by the arguments supporting the change and the results of any voting can also be published.

It prioritizes the different ongoing projects in the company

Large corporations often run hundreds of projects at any one time and at all levels: corporate, business unit and departmental. Some projects are temporary, others permanent. Some relate to efficiency, some to innovation, and others to a specific issue that has arisen within the company. All of them take up management time and the attention of company executives.

The EDC is no panacea for diminishing the number of projects in an organization. However if, say, three projects are attached to every point on the strategic alignment agenda, executives throughout the organization are able to know at the very least which of these projects have a high priority. This imperative is then known and supported by those at the top of the organization. The effect might well be that other slightly less-important projects just disappear.

It creates transparency and accountability for improvement projects

The projects 'hanging' in the CEO's virtual office have a definition, description, time-line, and allocated personnel. If the process is managed correctly, the status of the project will be regularly updated, and anyone anywhere in the company who is attached to the EDC will be able to look at it. In this situation, there can be no misunderstanding about who is accountable for bringing the project to a successful conclusion.

It allows the sharing of knowledge throughout the company on subjects involving improvement projects

In point 4, we described how the board is able to share a memorandum with a large group of managers. We have also outlined the ability to create transparency around projects emerging from the strategic alignment agenda. There is transparency both about the agenda and the projects. The fact that the strategic alignment agenda is the priority for the company as a whole means that in almost every corner of the corporation executives should be able to examine the status of the relevant projects. They might be able both to learn and to contribute. A prioritized form of knowledge sharing greatly improves the effectiveness of a large organization.

It clarifies the responsibilities and accountabilities of individual board members concerning the strategic alignment agenda

As already discussed, EDCs can be designed to have a CEO's office with separate buttons for individual management board members who have their own offices and information they want to share. This gives them the possibility of carrying out an operational dialogue with 'their' people. Whichever design or form is selected, it is clear that transparency about the agenda and accountability for the projects (including the president's or CFO's accountability) make it absolutely clear who is responsible for what. It is also evident which projects are being led by the CEO himself and where other executives are involved.

Of course, one risk of putting the CEO back in the middle of the operation is that he might tend to start micro-managing in areas that are clearly the responsibility of one of his colleagues. Managing by strategic pull and operational push is not only a question of adapting to a different management style, it also requires discipline in relation to what to do and what not to do. A well-designed EDC can be of great help in this regard.

It personalizes the leadership

Through the virtual CEO's office, leadership can be virtually present day in and day out and CEOs are able to share their concerns. The EDC is also a place where fear can be transformed into shared uncertainty, the importance of which is outlined in Chapter 7. Also, the CEO can react personally to any questions raised.

There are different ways of doing this. The CEO of AVEBE, an international agricultural company, organized his virtual dialogue in a specific way. First of all, he promised his people that they would get a personal answer within a maximum of seven days. Second, he introduced two virtual mailboxes and managers could decide which one to use. The first was a public one: the question as well as the CEO's answer was there for everyone to see. The second mailbox was closed: the question as well as the answer was between the individual and the CEO.

It allows the board's 'excitement' to be shared with key people

Again, we emphasize that management beyond control is a meritocratic process. CEOs have to earn their authority, and participants need to show what they are worth. These key individuals, who are so crucial to the company's future success, are people who want to be challenged, want to contribute, and want to be professionally stretched. For many of them being part of the inner circle is extremely rewarding.

Certainly, life at the top is not always easy, but every CEO knows that there are many moments of great excitement, full of adrenalin, gratification and importance. It is extremely rewarding to contribute to the progress of so many people, in so many countries. The excitement of being able to compete with the best in the industry, of making a social contribution, but also of carrying heavy responsibility, should be shared with the best and the brightest. People who can combine doing an excellent day-to-day job in their operating function with once in a while accepting the responsibility of an active part in the corporate dialogue are those who will appreciate having access to the exciting world of top management.

The process of managing beyond control

To summarize, managing beyond control is about aligning the organization's operating agenda with its strategic agenda. First, this requires continuous and up-to-date knowledge of the current organizational capabilities (measuring) and a clear understanding of organizational problems and priorities (the operating agenda). Second, the strategic agenda and operating agenda need to be brought in line with each other (matching), a procedure that needs to be repeated and monitored over time through a highly structured corporate dialogue (managing) between the CEO and a select group of key executives (Figure 6.3).

With measuring, matching and managing, a typical organization can create a highly interconnected operating arena. The strategic alignment process then takes place through focused, structured dialogue, guided by the strategic alignment agenda. The appropriate way to manage and institutionalize such a dialogue is to create an *executive dialogue centre* where the CEO calls the shots with regard to defining and managing the occasions and types of interaction. His motives for deciding what to tell people and how to interact will be based on two principles:

- There is more chance of success when talented executives are well informed and highly involved.
- There is no real accountability without transparency.

The interaction in the executive dialogue centre will make the operating arena transparent in the sense that:

- company executives will clearly understand the strategy and all operational processes;
- all company executives will be fully aware of their own and others' accountabilities.

Keeping the strategic alignment agenda permanently alive throughout the organization is instrumental to attaining alignment. It serves as the main guideline for creating and managing a highly effective, interconnected, TransCountable operating arena. In Part III, we will describe how to activate the full process and the roles of different executives in this alignment process, but first, in the next chapter, we take a step back to consider some of the principles underlying our approach.

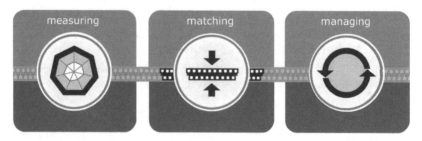

Figure 6.3 Managing beyond control

Lessons learned

- In order to get back into the middle of his corporation, the CEO can take advantage of the opportunities offered by an *executive dialogue centre* (EDC).
- Experience with companies has led to the development of a web-based executive dialogue centre for practical use. This is a custom-designed portal that facilitates communication and information exchange between the CEO and his key personnel. This is a custom-designed portal that facilitates communication and information exchange between the CEO and his key personnel.
- The EDC should be able to transmit facts and audio/video content, report feedback, and provide a rich forum for interaction.
- There are ten reasons for establishing an EDC:
  1 It generates clarity on what the company stands for.
  2 It facilitates the measuring, matching and managing process necessary to create strategic alignment.
  3 It keeps the strategic alignment agenda alive.
  4 It improves the quality of the company's decision making.
  5 It prioritizes the different ongoing projects in the company.
  6 It creates transparency and accountability for improvement projects.
  7 It allows the sharing of knowledge throughout the company on subjects involving improvement projects.
  8 It clarifies the responsibilities and accountabilities of individual board members concerning the strategic alignment agenda.
  9 It personalizes the leadership.
  10 It allows the board's 'excitement' to be shared with key people.

7

The Fundamentals:
A Mindset for Pull and Push

New insights are required to enable management beyond control. In this context, 'insights' means having both a theoretical framework and a set of reasoned opinions about the organizational dynamics. After all, you can only convince others if you are convinced yourself. Unless you believe in most of the principles supporting a pull and push management style, it will be difficult to live up to your conviction that creating strategic alignment through dialogue is the way to go.

A CEO will only be able to manage beyond control if he is convinced that openness pays. This chapter provides a foundation, or a comfort level, for *management beyond control*, which will lead to better alignment of strategy and execution. But we also intend the chapter to show how CEOs can create sufficient risk-taking behaviour in their key personnel, avoid overmotivating them and yet still offer tremendous inspiration.

Four pillars

The principles of the management system that we introduce in this book are based on four fundamentals, which we call the four 'pillars' (Figure 7.1):

1 *Strategy formulation and execution can emerge out of complex circumstances, if we moderate our urge to control.*

2 *Managed individual freedom can stimulate corporate commitment and responsibility, and reinforces the acceptance of authority.*

3 *Transparency and accountability are corporate assets rather than corporate or social obligations. They should be well-defined (TransCountability), 'felt', measured and lived by.*

4 *Permanent, well-structured corporate dialogue transforms the ever-present fear of failure into a stimulating type of uncertainty, which creates energy, a quest for innovation and a culture of respect.*

Managing complexity is about letting go

Most people will say that they favour simple things over complex ones. Generally, the term 'complexity' conjures up a vision of

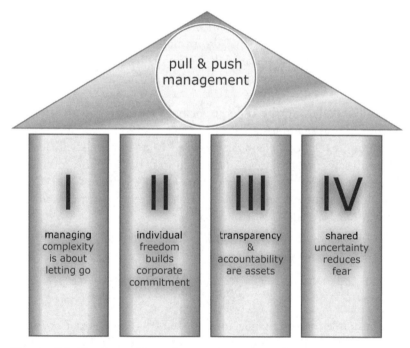

Figure 7.1 The four pillars of management by pull and push

difficulty, complication and lack of control. In organizations, we look for ways of reducing consumers' personal preferences to a limited set of intelligible segments; we streamline production chains to eliminate redundancy and reach a higher degree of optimization; and we reduce organization charts to PowerPoint slides that attempt to depict the firm's connectivity.

Yet, as individuals, we often value highly complex phenomena over simple ones. For example, most people would prefer a holiday visiting remote rainforests to the clean simplicity of staying home. Similarly, many people value Johann Sebastian Bach's music over Philip Glass's minimalism; and most people place a higher value on a meal that includes many select ingredients than one consisting of a sandwich.

What is at play here is a distinction between the complexity of a given phenomenon and the nature of our experience. When experiencing food, music or nature, we have varying degrees of education and training that influence our valuation of the aesthetic inherent in the complex exterior. For example, while Bach's music may be exceedingly convoluted in its composition, we somehow experience the simplicity of the mathematical principles at play behind the complex façade.

Consequently, when we say that we object to complexity in an organization or a business model, it is often the *direct experience* of that complexity to which we are reacting. It can be argued that this reaction occurs because we lack the intellectual and intuitive tools to experience the simple principles behind the complex phenomena.

In organizations, we implicitly believe that complex causes lead to complex phenomena. This is an important issue, as we cannot reasonably manage complex causes. The distinction between our experience and the objective complexity of the phenomenon is fundamental. In past decades substantial progress has been made in understanding how simple principles lead to complex phenomena and how order emerges within complexity. This insight is fundamental to understanding how organizations work and to leveraging complexity in order to manage companies for optimal performance and competitive advantage.

So why can't we let go?

Why do we want to control our organizations? Setting aside for a moment personal motives of power, it is surely because we believe that imposing our will is necessary for the organization to achieve its goals; centralized control is the source of order in the system. The roots of this belief lie in our education, which is still largely grounded in the beliefs of the late eighteenth-century Enlightenment.

These early scientific insights created a true sense of excitement that humans were at last becoming able to predict nature and mould it to their will. Large-scale engineering was born and the Industrial Revolution sought to organize labour like the cogs and pins of a machine. The central paradigm of this worldview is direct causality: everything that happens does so because of something else. By implication, this means that if you control the cause, you can influence the effect. Looking back, this approach was highly successful, creating unsurpassed material wealth, at least in the industrialized countries.

Nevertheless, the organizational systems that confront us today are less straightforward, and the deficiencies of our methods and beliefs are becoming apparent. This is evident in the difficulty that companies have in finding the optimal organizational form, leading many to resort to almost continual change.

It is useless for leaders who need to deliver concrete results simply to cry over spilt milk. They must accept that *linear* causality is increasingly unhelpful as the source of order and discover another source, compatible with the inherent complexity of their business. In fact, another source does exist. The new discipline of complexity purports to understand and describe order in highly *nonlinear* systems. These are systems where the overall behaviour of the system is determined by multiple feedback loops on many levels, rather than linearly from a central cause. Many real-life corporate systems fit this pattern.

Order for free

What is the alternative source of order in 'complex adaptive systems', as they are called in the jargon of complexity science?[1] In fact, what is a complex adaptive system (CAS)? It is a system of semi-independent agents that interact more or less randomly, influencing each other's behaviour. The agents evaluate when their interactions have left them better or worse off according to a *fitness criterion*. As an example, think of a group of door-to-door salespeople who know that selling more is a good thing and who randomly meet colleagues to exchange ideas and gossip.

The right combination of a fitness criterion (more sales) and random encounters is what leads to the nonlinear growth of order in a complex adaptive system. As in a neural network, the combination of a fitness criterion and random feedback loops has become a highly efficient information-processing system. It turns out to be much more efficient than the traditional method of having each salesperson report back to a central marketing entity.

To better understand this interaction between the two key ingredients – fitness criterion and random encounters – imagine that you are a semi-independent agent in a complex adaptive system. Perhaps you are an employee of a large multinational corporation, an amino acid, an element in an ecosystem or even a stockbroker. You are bouncing around, randomly interacting with other agents in the system. The one thing you 'know' is what is 'good': the fitness criterion.

Most often the fitness criterion is connected to survival in a wider sense, such as the long-term profitability of the corporation you are in, survival of the species you are a part of, and so on. In every random interaction you receive information about how your actions enhance or decrease your fitness through your contribution to the system. Your fitness is not absolute, but is relative to the fitness of other agents in the system around you.

In this way you 'learn' to adapt your behaviour to increase your fitness. This web of very local and random interactions, which occurs without any explicit directives, leads to an increase in the fitness of the entire system. This happens because your behaviour contributes to the fitness of the system in a positive way and is linked to that system as a whole through the feedback in the interactions. Contrast this with a mechanistic view, where you wait for an explicit instruction for every move, either deduced from a rule or given by another agent in the system (i.e. the boss).

To illustrate this in another way, imagine you are taking a walk in a rugged landscape. The goal of the walk is to find the deepest valley; this is your chosen fitness criterion in this particular case. One strategy could be to walk downhill from every point. This will certainly achieve the goal of reaching a deep point, but it will be unclear whether this is the deepest point or merely a local pit. Another strategy could be to walk downhill but randomly change direction at a certain frequency and then compare the altitude. This will avoid you becoming stuck in a local valley because the random deviation from the downhill path could very well send you back uphill in some direction. However, too much changing of direction will result in purposeless wandering.

The key to success in complex adaptive systems is to strike the right balance between order (always walking downhill) and disorder (random changes of direction). Given the right feedback mechanisms, a system 'far from equilibrium, poised at the edge of order and disorder' will spontaneously organize itself in a sustainable and efficient way. What the 'right' balance is depends on the circumstances, and it is the role of leaders to comprehend enough about the dynamics of complexity to design the right balance into their organization. Finding the right balance is not straightforward, as it depends critically on the organizational problem at hand. This is represented by the 'ruggedness of the landscape'. Leaders will manage the dynamics more effectively, however, if they understand the principles of finding nonanalytical solutions.

In practical examples of complex systems, whether they are scheduling problems for field crews or logistical optimizations, the tool used to fine-tune the system is computer simulation. This is not an analytical model with equations to be solved, but a brute-force simulation of the interactions of the agents in the system. These simulations allow managers to understand how to 'tune' the system in order to achieve the desired emergent behaviour.

What can we learn from complexity theory?

Unfortunately there are no 'eight easy steps' for using complexity or 'twelve key rules' to apply, as in so much management literature.

Rather, complexity is a fundamental evolution of our mental model of how systems work, one that seems to explain the behaviour of stock markets, ecosystems and large firms more closely than the traditional approach.

Leaders need to glean the following from complexity theory:

- *Appreciate the holistic nature of a system and the emergence of system-level properties.* Like the well-worn example of a butterfly flapping its wings in Rio de Janeiro causing a storm in Chicago, small causes can have large and nonlinear effects. So it is important to bear in mind that a change in one part of the corporate system may have an unexpected effect on another part, making feedback and monitoring all the more important.
- *Develop a nondirective style of leadership.* The role of the leader is to be involved and challenged, but not to micro-manage. He must set the vision and then provide the operating arena – the intent, objectives, resources and interactions – that will allow the organization and its people to flourish.
- *Create clear fitness criteria for the organization (goals).* Give it a sense of purpose, a common cause. This will allow people to know what is 'good' for the organization, what will help it survive. If it doesn't have transparency in this area, it will not be able to gauge how well it is doing compared with its competitors and in light of changes in its environment.
- *Design redundancy into the process.* Removing all duplication and overlap in an organization will severely curtail the density of interactions within it. Of course, having too much overlap creates turf wars and inefficiency; but since it runs so deeply against the grain of our management culture, it is important to emphasize that an appropriate level of duplication and overlap is essential.
- *Have just enough rules to limit randomness in the organization to a level where it is fruitful, but not so many as to put the organization into a state of equilibrium.* The organization will function at its best when it is poised at the edge of disorder. There needs to be a balance between constraints and freedoms, a concept that is addressed in more detail below.

Eric Beinhocker of McKinsey also argues that the edge of chaos is the place to be:

> Unlike creatures in nature, we are not blind, passive players in the evolutionary game. Through the sciences of complexity, we can come to understand how evolution works, the tricks it has up its sleeve, and the skills needed to survive in a complex world. If we do so, we may be able to harness one of the most powerful forces of all: evolution will then be the wave we ride to new levels of creativity and innovation rather than the tide that washes over us.[2]

Individual freedom supports commitment

Humans don't only need a spirit of inclusiveness. Physical as well as psychological liberty is probably the ultimate achievement for most intelligent human beings. As we described above, managing in complex systems requires some limitations on freedom, namely the creation of clear fitness criteria and a corporate purpose: a common cause shared throughout the organization. We need limits so that we don't wander around blindly and randomly looking for our next steps.

People will accept limits, as long as they know why these are necessary. The actual benefit of having some kind of limitation on one's freedom of action is extensively argued in the work of the late Oxford professor and philosopher Sir Isaiah Berlin. While individuals naturally desire freedom, there is still a need to provide processes and structures; otherwise society (and organizations) would descend into anarchy. Freedom needs to go together with responsibility: total freedom for one person or group always limits the freedom of someone else.

> A man on an island – Robinson Crusoe – is totally free, until Man Friday arrives. After that reciprocal obligations begin . . . The bird may think that it would fly more freely in a vacuum: but it would not – it would fall. There is no society without some authority: and that limits liberty.

People are willing to accept limitations on their individual freedom as long as they acknowledge the authority of those setting the boundaries; as long as they accept that those people 'know what is best not only for themselves but also for me' – in other words, as long as power and authority are not separate. Then a foundation can be formed to create responsibility for the common cause and the possibility of being included in society and organizations.

If we translate Berlin's reasoning into the operating arena, it is easy to recognize its significance. Free-spirited, talented executives favour maximum freedom in order to excel, apply their intelligence (come up with new combinations) and use their potential. They consider themselves Human Capital, as does their company. But it is they who choose to be part of a particular organization, appreciating and accepting its defined intent, its potent objectives, and also the degree of involvement, interaction and corporate support for taking initiatives. If this acceptance happens, CEOs have earned their power. Authority then comes naturally in a culture of freedom and respect because people feel engaged. This engagement creates a natural platform for the alignment of strategy and execution.

Transparency and accountability are assets

As we have already mentioned, a lack of transparency, accountability and integrity was *the* symptom that proves a system failure, with fatal consequences for many companies at the end of the twentieth and the beginning of the twenty-first centuries. In Chapter 2, we discussed the absolute necessity for more transparency and better-applied accountability. The creation of transparency for, and accountability towards, all 'owners' is a prerequisite for a modern, open and 'human' enterprise.

This is not only because, as Charles Handy argues, a company can hardly be considered to be 'owned' *just* by its shareholders, since

it is a strange type of ownership. The 'thing' which they own mostly consists of people. Owning people, no matter how well you treat them, is considered wrong in every other part of life.[3]

It is also because creating transparency and accountability is the basis for creating a culture of integrity and respect.

Transparency and accountability in complex systems: The human factor

Earlier in this chapter, we have seen how in simulated complex systems the dual forces of clear goal setting (that is, the fitness criterion) and a high density of interactions can lead to increasing order, under the appropriate circumstances. If we make the assumption that organizations can be largely characterized as complex adaptive systems in their behaviour, how can the interaction between the elements of the system – the employees, departments or functions – be optimized to take advantage of the dynamics of complexity?

Another way of putting this question is: Under what circumstances do human 'agents' (as opposed to the somewhat sterile 'semi-independent agents') most willingly strive towards a common goal, and how can we stimulate high-value-adding interactions?

Of course, we can get people to strive towards a common goal by ordering or coercing them, but that won't necessarily be particularly productive. In contrast, if we engage staff in the goal-setting process itself, there will be full ownership as well as the additional benefit of tapping into the intelligence distributed throughout the organization.

But a transparent goal-setting process is not enough to harness the order available through complexity. It is also necessary for those in the organization to be *accountable* for delivering on the goals set, and if possible even to adapt or evolve the goals themselves. Once again, accountability can be achieved in a directive or coercive fashion, but at the price of the quality of the interactions.

So, from a complexity perspective, a culture of transparency and accountability conducted in a spirit of inclusiveness is the necessary foundation for human 'agents' to be able to engage in creative interactions, thereby leading to a higher degree of order than would otherwise be available. Effectively this entails using the knowledge embedded in the organization and leveraging that knowledge to full advantage. Better and more effective use of knowledge compared with the competition is an important source of competitive advantage and will create better-functioning business models and therefore superior return on all capital invested, including human capital.

This is why we should deal with transparency and accountability in terms of productivity enhancement rather than organizational control. Transparency and accountability are indeed corporate assets.

Shared uncertainty reduces fear

We have discussed liberty and inclusiveness as two elements that we want our talented people to experience. But they also need to be free from fear, such as the fear of making mistakes or even the fear of corporate failure. Fear stifles and inhibits creativity. While it is impossible to create the complete absence of fear, reducing fear by transforming it into shared uncertainty is the fourth pillar on which we build management beyond control.

Although some degree of fear or anxiety reflects a primitive mechanism that enables us to react swiftly to danger, over a long period fear is debilitating. Lars Weisaeth, professor of psychotraumatology at the University of Oslo, explains:

> *Research shows that as our anxiety increases, we begin to lose our ability to understand, remember and think in terms of actual probabilities. We become irrational and believe that the calamity will befall us alone, however small the risk may be. At the same time, we are often skillful at suppressing and denying anything we don't wish to acknowledge.*[4]

Research by the sociologist Niklas Luhmann also suggests that people don't function well with too much fear, but that they do function well with risk – as long as they understand it.[5]

For example, if you are in a crowded airport and you know there have been warnings of potential terrorist attacks, you will feel fear because you are unable to assess the risk you face. However, if you can see that everything is extremely well organized, there are a large number of police around and there are warning signs and security cameras, you get the feeling that the authorities are approaching the danger in a structured, professional way. You and the authorities are sharing the risks.

Translating the above example into large corporations is not difficult. If leadership is not in the middle of the company, fear readily enters the psyche of middle managers – especially if things are getting rough, the company is under attack, profits are falling and ratios are such that banks are starting to ask questions. If the leaders are not visible, managers start questioning their authority and fear and cynicism starts to creep in. In contrast, if leaders are at the middle of the company and are seen to be sharing the uncertainty, they will gain respect and people will feel more comfortable.

Inspiration is important and being motivated is necessary, but don't underestimate the risk of *overmotivating* because this kills managers' risk-taking capacity. CEOs who don't leave room for doubt close the door on alternative and better solutions.

A culture of fear, avoidance of risk and maintenance of the *status quo* stifle too many large, bureaucratic corporations. In contrast, history shows us that it pays off to face the enemy and fight for a purpose. Managers should feel dignified and competent, and should aspire to more than just maintaining the *status quo* in order to keep what they have.

Successful CEOs are great communicators; they have a vision that they can translate into a common cause. Look inside a successful company and you will see engagement; you will see managers wanting to take risks. Managers who are afraid and unwilling to take any risks will achieve nothing.

Nevertheless, the best CEOs recognize that a latent fear of failure often stifles executives and creates an atmosphere of complacency, thereby maintaining the *status quo* and resisting change. Leaders have to find a *new* system of transforming fear into risk-sharing.

This is where *dialogue* fits in. Dialogue is the vehicle that creates focus and turns fear into shared uncertainty. Dialogue between the leaders and their 'troops' can be about many things: the common cause; aligning strategy and execution; organizational capabilities;

the strategic alignment agenda; improvement projects; competition; and anything that can help the company successfully conquer the future. If, through dialogue, you understand the nature of the risks and what is being done to mitigate them, your fear will be reduced, and the entire organization will be energized and focused.

People follow behaviour, not strategy, and conviction influences behaviour. Believing in and displaying a convinced opinion that pull and push management leads to the alignment of strategy and execution makes it possible for any CEO to have the courage of his convictions.

Lessons learned

- We need to understand the dynamics of organizations through both a theoretical framework and a set of reasoned opinions, in order to make the case for managing beyond control and creating strategic alignment through dialogue.
- Management beyond control is management by pull and push. Four principles function as the four 'pillars', i.e. fundamentals for this philosophy:

  1 Strategy formulation and execution can emerge out of complex circumstances, if we moderate our urge to control.

  2 Managed individual freedom can stimulate corporate commitment and responsibility, and even reinforce the acceptance of authority.

  3 Transparency and accountability are potential corporate assets rather than obligations. They should be well understood, 'felt', measured and lived by.

  4 Permanent, well-structured corporate dialogue transforms the ever-present fear of failure into a stimulating type of uncertainty, which creates energy, a quest for innovation and a culture of respect.
- Complexity theory presents us with some important imperatives:

  1 Appreciate the holistic nature of a system and the potential for answers and solutions to emerge from within that system.

  2 Develop a nondirective style of leadership.

3 Create clear fitness criteria for the organization (goals).
4 Design redundancy into the process.
5 Have just enough rules to limit randomness in the organization to a level where it is fruitful, but not so many as to put the organization into a state of equilibrium.

- Transparency and accountability are crucial drivers for the creation of a culture of respect. A company that possesses a high degree of 'TransCountability' is well equipped to be strategically aligned. Therefore, we can consider transparency and accountability as corporate assets.
- Individual physical and mental freedom is the ultimate desire of intelligent managers. But individuals accept limitations on their freedom as long as they understand them and acknowledge the authority of those who have set them. Authority can be created through dialogue.
- Fear stifles and inhibits creativity. CEOs are able to share uncertainty through dialogue and openness, which helps to diminish the fear that things will turn out badly.

Part III

Managing Alignment Leading, Rewarding and Reporting

Parts I and II outlined our approach for the leading of large corporations, namely management beyond control. This should be done with integrity, transparency and accountability. Creating an operating arena in which the strategic alignment agenda can be managed through dialogue will increase the possibility of aligning strategy and execution.

As we have seen, a CEO needs the commitment of his full leadership team and the collaboration of his talent base to create such a company. Success lies in gaining the cooperation of all these competent, engaged managers, with their example-setting and their integrity, at all levels of the organization.

But what is day-to-day life like in a company managed by pull and push? In Part III, we consider different functions within the organization: the CEO, naturally, but also heads of finance, human resources and communications, to give concrete examples of what is really involved in strategic alignment through corporate dialogue.

8

The Chief Executive Officer
Believer-in-Chief

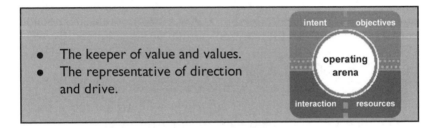

- The keeper of value and values.
- The representative of direction and drive.

intent   objectives

operating
arena

interaction   resources

The overall responsibility for managing beyond control lies fairly and squarely with the CEO. He can be seen as the key to unlocking the corporate wisdom contained within the organization.

For management beyond control, the ideal leader is financially and mentally free and thrives on the constructive aspects of criticism. He not only claims that open organizations are inherently more effective, but truly believes it. This includes accepting – indeed, welcoming – any challenges to his own ideas and plans from his people and being willing to consider these challenges impartially.

'His people' not only means key executives throughout the organization, but also his own leadership team. We have to recognize that, as Robert McNamara wrote recently:

in every large institution, fundamental but highly controversial issues often are not surfaced, and debate at the highest levels is not forced, because it's recognized by the chief executive, or his associates, that to do so will split the executive group. The leader's responsibility is to force debate on the most fundamental issues confronting the organization, even though it may cause resentment and tear the organization apart, at least temporarily.[1]

We realize, of course, that in many cases the person we describe represents an entire leadership team rather than a single individual. The CEO has various roles: he is both the 'keeper of *values*' and the 'keeper of *value*'. He also embodies the direction of the organization, being *the* executive responsible for the formulation and execution of corporate strategy, and ensuring it is permanently monitored for potential adaptation, if necessary.

Although disciplined thinking along the lines of industry analyses and competitive business models is the starting point of a sound corporate strategy, it also requires a strong input of knowledge from within the organization through a tough process of testing, failure, success and feedback dialogue.

This process requires a leadership team that is strong enough not only to formulate the required strategy, including setting a tough agenda, but also to guarantee its execution in order to create the necessary value. In addition, it also needs a CEO with a deep conviction that incorporating the often very practical knowledge lying deep within the organization is not merely vital to winning ownership of the strategic alignment agenda, but is also instrumental in arriving at the best available agenda.

Intent: Being an internal and external role model

As we have stressed, people follow behaviour, not strategy. Any CEO needs to remember that the organization keeps a close watch on what he does, rather than on what he says. It is therefore very important that his behaviour and actions be consistent with his message. If the CEO stresses that the organization needs to be transparent and accountable, his actions must reflect these principles. Key personnel know how the management board functions: for example, if the board stops meeting every one or two weeks, or if the chief, chairman or

CEO starts regularly missing meetings, the organization begins to fall apart, at least in the eyes of intelligent people.

Let's not forget that a leader's actual behaviour reveals more about the level of commitment and discipline within a company than any internal or external press coverage of the firm. The CEO must accept that openness, honesty and transparency are part of his responsibility. Being a role model covers important aspects like how the CEO supervises his own team – and how intensively – as well as simple but telling behaviour such as whether office doors are often locked on the executive floor.

In 2001, Ben Verwaayen became the new CEO of British Telecom. He felt that an effective CEO should follow three basic rules:

- Set the right tone.
- Define and follow the right agenda.
- Make sure the best people surround you.

He defined tone broadly:

- Don't position yourself as CEO outside (above) your company, but try to be one among equals; this applies to all top executives.
- Create a culture of individual accountability (be specific).
- Embrace meritocracy.
- Be customer-centred.

Verwaayen realized that it was likely his subordinates were going to look to him as their role model. He was fully aware of the importance of all aspects that symbolized the kind of CEO he was going to be. People would be looking for a mixture of 'big' and 'small' signals. One of the many actions he took was to abandon the executive elevator, which used to bring his predecessor to his office. He also started having lunch with his fellow managers instead of using the executive dining room. He publicized his email address so that customers could complain directly to him: this meant that he had to answer and take action on several hundred emails each week. The challenge was to find a balance between avoiding micro-managing on the one hand and getting involved by taking and displaying personal accountability on the other hand. In addition to reaching into the core of the operation himself, Verwaayen made sure that his senior executives also got the message.

One day he made his top executives go out on the road with an average BT employee. Every single senior executive had to formulate one area of improvement that had arisen during that day. Each of them had to take personal responsibility (accountability) for tackling and solving the issue encountered.

Clear and visible symbols demonstrate how to set the tone to all stakeholders, inside the organization as well as externally. And on the subject of agenda-setting, Verwaayen is quite unequivocal: 'Make sure that there is a clear and common definition of what success stands for in this company'.

Talented people want to be led with authority, by CEOs with a clear 'corporate story', and by leaders with a vision, an agenda, a drive for perfect execution and a passion for results. By focusing on managing alignment, and by using the pull and push style of management, the TransCountable CEO can earn this authority. Most likely such a CEO will have a vivid and detailed picture in his own mind of how the company will look a few years down the line.

Let's examine the example of a company three years after it began to be managed by pull and push. The CEO is taking stock of where the company stands:

'I have always perceived the business environment as very complex. Growth opportunities are more and more local and niche-based. This requires us to leverage our execution capability, placing responsibilities low down in the company while developing some key capabilities globally. Our company has done quite well in its respective markets and our cost levels have dropped. Our stakeholders (employees, consumers, shareholders, as well as the communities we operate in) have become more and more demanding. They expect us to be an exciting company to work for, to ensure that our profits and growth remain sustainable, and to make the company a responsible partner in our society.

'I have felt wonderfully supported by my people in all these developments. The executive dialogue centre (some call it the chairman's portal) that we started using right after my appointment has proved an exciting tool for communicating with my people. I get great input from them, and in turn they feel that there is more focus in the company. It has really helped that we have defined a small number of distinct items on our – and therefore my – CEO agenda. People always know what is on my mind and act accordingly.

'The company has enormously reduced the number of projects that were going on. Now mainly those projects that have a direct link with the strategic – and thus my – agenda receive funding and the best people.

'I feel we are permanently unlocking the corporate wisdom embedded deep down in the organization, and yet I feel more in control and better able to provide direction, without the temptation of micro-managing my people. I feel that I stand closer to our key people. In fact, I have hard data to prove it. Profits are up and our alignment score has improved considerably from the situation it was in when I was appointed.'

The above story exemplifies what it means to have a clear vision about the future of your company in all its facets, and how important it is to try to make that vision as explicit as possible. If you can't dream it, you can't do it. But if you aren't specific, you won't be able to execute and implement the vision.

On the other hand, we should realize that no two individuals are the same, and this also applies to CEOs. In the end, it always comes down to the values and personality that a particular person brings to the job. Boards will appreciate and accept individuality as long as the competencies necessary to fulfil the task are present and, we argue, the CEO in charge profoundly believes in building a company managed by pull and push.

Steering the company in the right direction

We have argued that the prime responsibility of any CEO is guiding his company towards superior returns, while ensuring competitiveness. Value will then be created for shareholders, customers and employees. This means that money is made, customers are happy, employees are content, markets are served and there is no damage to society. As the CEO is also the person responsible for sustaining the corporate dialogue, he must convince his (outside) board as well as any stakeholders that he feels responsible for guaranteeing the company's integrity and transparency. Then, investors, employees and all business partners with an interest in the company don't have to fear sudden surprises.

As complexity increases, managing financial results alone won't do. Managing the alignment between strategy and execution and defining the operating arena enable the CEO to take positive control of the direction and speed of the company. The fact that the CEO has created clarity about the organizational values, and the framework and boundaries within which the leadership team wants the corporation to operate worldwide, allows him to let go. He can manage beyond control. He is able to put his stamp on the execution of the corporate story, and to make sure that the company is operating in the way he wants and in accord with his long-term vision. The CEO finds that he is able to make a difference by embracing the corporate dialogue:

- By taking responsibility for the corporate story and corporate goal setting, including corporate values.
- By creating a strategic alignment agenda by matching strategic and operational priorities through dialogue.

- By keeping both the story and agenda permanently alive throughout the company worldwide.
- By listening intently to what people within his company think – about the strategy, about the execution and maybe about themselves.
- By persuading his key personnel to assess the capability of the organization to fulfil the company's values and strategic alignment agenda.
- By making himself accountable for the things he will do personally on this strategic alignment agenda.
- By helping managers start the process of alignment and managing by pull and push in their specific divisions, business units and departments.

In Chapter 4, we quoted Novartis chief Daniel Vasella describing how the prospect of failure might keep a CEO awake at night. This is a normal human fear. Nevertheless, a culture based on corporate dialogue is able to take away a considerable part of that fear. Then, a CEO will not have to carry the uncertainty of success on his own or with his leadership team; it will be shared much further down in the organization.

This sharing is accomplished with the strategic alignment agenda as the backbone, and the strategic alignment agenda is formulated through structured dialogue. The board's issues are combined with the priorities that came bottom-up from within the organization. In this way, the strategic agenda combines with the operational agenda and become the strategic alignment agenda.

This is not a 'soft' process. You might feel that, if you start a dialogue with large groups of executives within your organization, the culture might become overly democratic and decisions will take too long. However, decisions don't have to be taken by majority vote just because you involve a large group of executives. All that is required is for decisions to be explained, and if necessary defended, especially if a majority of executives have different ideas.

Today this can take place without losing speed. Digitization has helped to build different infrastructures, so that structured dialogue can be digitally organized. For instance, with an executive dialogue centre (EDC), a CEO can involve hundreds of managers without sacrificing momentum.

> Take the example of a large multinational firm with more than 100 000 employees spread over many countries. The management board has to make a short-term decision that they have already discussed with their divisional managers, but they would like to make sure, by involving a much larger group, that all operational issues have been examined and that a large base of support exists for the final decision. The CEO decides to use the EDC to communicate directly with his talent base, comprising approximately 1500 managers. He sends out the following message: 'We have to act quickly, in four weeks' time. There are a couple of proposals on the table. I want to share the alternatives with you and get a feeling for your ideas.'
>
> Managers enter the EDC, read and/or download the proposal and its alternatives, and then react. At the end of four weeks, having achieved a response rate of, say, 75%, the management board decide they can make a quality decision, as the base of key executives will feel involved and the tough consequences resulting from the decision might gain enough support. It will be much easier for the divisional managers to carry the decision through than if the company had not managed through dialogue.

Even if the board decides to act differently from what the majority has proposed, a CEO will still be able to execute that decision without losing authority. As we have already stressed, human beings want to be led by someone they respect. They want leaders who make the necessary decisions, and even if the final result is different from what they might have wanted, they will accept it as long as the arguments are shared. Managers know that power should be in the hands of the CEO, so that power and authority are aligned. Let's look at a fictitious example.

A company is considering investing in projects to strengthen its role as an active social player in the world community. The leadership team has discussed different approaches and possibilities and wants to formulate a final strategy at the beginning of the following year. Using the executive dialogue centre, the CEO decides to involve his identified key executive base of 1300 managers worldwide. The following dilemma questions will be put to the managers, who will be asked to respond within ten days before a management board meeting takes place to discuss the issue:

- Dilemma question 1. Our company, consistent with its conviction that it should be a responsible partner in its community, should continue spending money on social causes.
- Dilemma question 2. Our company, consistent with its conviction that it should be a responsible partner in its community, should carry out corporate-wide social programmes.
- Dilemma question 3. Our company, consistent with its conviction that it should be a responsible partner in its community, should encourage local operating companies to budget for community-friendly activities and decide locally how to spend the money.

The outcome of the dilemma questions was surprising: 60% of the 1300 managers favoured local projects, while only 40% were in favour of a corporate-wide programme. Interestingly enough, 48% of the female participants opted for a local approach, while 52% favoured a corporate programme. Looking at the 'high potentials', the corporate approach was favoured by as many as 53%.

These data were reported at the management board meeting. During the meeting, the board opted for a corporate-wide approach giving the organization the ability to work with an international children's organization helping less-developed countries, with activities that were very much in line with its normal business practices.

After the board discussion, all 1300 people were sent the results of the dilemma scan. They were told that the board had used their input in making its decision, that the decision and its consequences would be announced to the outside world at the beginning of the following year, and that shortly before the announcement a further explanation would be given to the 1300 managers. As things still had to be worked out and certain levels of confidentiality were necessary, more details could not be given at that time. A few months later, 12 hours before the press conference, the CEO reported digitally to the group of 1300. He explained why the board had decided on a corporate plan instead of local activities.

Let's consider the position of a CEO managing the triangle of customer value creation, employee value creation and shareholder value creation. His ambition would be to increase the size of the whole triangle over time. Employees want a good salary and a reasonable work–life balance, shareholders want greater dividends and higher profits (resulting in a high share price), and customers want the best quality and the lowest price. There are some obvious tensions between these different wishes and objectives. Nevertheless, over time, one hopes that the CEO will build a company that creates more value for all these stakeholders and therefore increases the size of the triangle.

However, the world does not grow smoothly and in total balance. There could be changes in the industry or bad economic conditions. Consequently, the company might need to emphasize only the financial side of the triangle, taking such actions as increasing margins and monitoring costs, so that for a couple of years there will be no investment in the corporate infrastructure, product innovation or management development programmes. Through the executive dialogue centre, the CEO can share the new agenda and explain that if the company is to survive it has to make some drastic changes. He could even share the dilemma of what is to be done: 'We need to cut costs by 10%. We have two alternatives. We could spread the budget cuts throughout the organization, or we could cut overhead support or find other solutions. What would be your preferred option and why? What can you personally do within your own arena to cut costs?'

Objectives: Goals that hit home and please people

As we have discussed, managing alignment and measuring and managing the operating arena contribute more to the sustainability and future success of a company than merely managing the financial results. Nevertheless, it is evident that setting and monitoring objectives remains an important part of every modern CEO's role. The following areas need to be considered:

- What are the objectives?
- Where are they derived from?
- Do they match the managers' personal agendas?
- How do we establish ownership of the objectives?
- How do we specify accountability?
- How do we create transparency?
- How do we tie-in reward systems?

Goals that hit home

Executing the strategy means formulating the agenda. We have described this agenda-setting process extensively in earlier chapters. In a modern company, ownership is established through some form of institutionalized dialogue. The agenda leads to the formulation of objectives and the establishment of key performance indicators representing the objectives. It should be quite evident that these 'cold' parameters are crucial in guiding the organization towards sustainable profitability.

The key performance indicators will make it possible to monitor continuously financial, customer, employee, structural, relationship (e.g. business partners) and societal value creation or value destruction. The CEO will play the crucial role in setting the tone for these objectives. At the end of the day, he is the one creating a sense of urgency for ensuring that the new yardsticks, like the organizational capability parameters, have equal importance to the traditional, mostly output-oriented measures used within the company. Are the key performance indicators supported and owned throughout the company? Are relevant pieces of information shared with different stakeholders by, for example, including them in the accounts? Are they made part of the reward system by which the company's executives and managers are rewarded and promoted?

This brings us to the 'warm' throughput side of objective setting.

Goals that please people

The alignment score helps measure the status of a company's capacity for alignment over time. The question raised in the northeast corner of the capacity for alignment model (see Figure 4.4) concerns the strength and ownership of the company's objectives: how potent are the objectives? We have argued that an effective leadership team makes sure that, in addition to the strategic 'pull' coming from the top, there is an organizational 'push' from deep within the organization. This will be the result of the alignment process, including involvement in agenda-setting, transparency and accountability around improvement projects and the functioning of the EDC.

The score for the 'objectives' quadrant in the model is based on two categories emerging from the 39 categories forming the operating arena: compelling objectives and personal accountability. These are the determining factors in the key people's assessment of the quality of the objectives. Again, the CEO will be the driving force behind the creation of a company where managers are held accountable for measurable objectives – the prerequisite for a meritocratic culture. If potent objectives go hand in hand with such a culture, the company is in an excellent position to create maximum engagement. Once more, we see the CEO as the keeper of structures and values.

A company managed by pull and push is more flexible, less bureaucratic, and has more positive tension and a greater feeling of ownership from its managers. This does not mean that all employees have to work 80 hours a week, but it does mean that they are made accountable for their own projects and know that their colleagues are also accountable. This helps in attracting, developing and retaining the best people, a challenge for even the best-performing companies. In creating an institutionalized dialogue with the real talent and asking them what the organizational capability should be, even in relation to such areas as benefit-and-reward systems, you create a culture of respect and accountability that fosters staff retention.

Therefore, it is the CEO's responsibility to make sure that there is a culture of transparency and accountability within the organization; not only in the sense that it is open, but also that people are being held accountable. If they don't live up to their accountability, steps will be taken. And don't forget that managers will watch closely whether their leaders practise what they preach.

It is important for the CEO to realize that managing by pull and push is not always a comfortable exercise and not everyone will like it. For years, managers have been rewarded on a combination of seniority, loyalty and attaining purely financial objectives. Now, in an age where transparency, accountability and integrity have come to be on equal terms with result orientation, a whole generation of managers educated during the last 25 years has had to make considerable adjustments. This is particularly so since, as we have shown in earlier chapters, business principles like integrity and other qualitative aspects can be measured consistently over time and made part of a company's key performance indicators. Furthermore, it should be evident that if achieving sustained profitability is dependent on strategic alignment as well as financial performance, then managers must be rewarded in accordance with their performance on both sides of the equation.

Resources: Making managers unlock people's potential

Consider the southeast corner of the model measuring strategic alignment: the company's resources. The owners of the corporation have entrusted the CEO to get the maximum out of his available resources in order to create superior returns. Although we have a tendency to talk about, and measure, returns on financial and physical resources, it is evident that returns on *human* resources are the starting point of many results.

The CEO should not only encourage a culture in which the organization facilitates its people by making available hard physical resources (offices, funding, IT, etc.), but he should also ensure that the softer types of resources are at hand. Talented people need to be inspired to go the extra mile, to be stimulated, to receive feedback, to be encouraged to take initiatives, to be unafraid to make mistakes, to look for opportunities and not to be held back unnecessarily – in other words, they should be given every assistance to enable them to excel within the boundaries of the strategic alignment agenda.

A CEO tries to create an atmosphere that encourages bosses in the organization to foster employee commitment by continually giving full support to their people. Talented people can make a huge contribution to the alignment process by getting involved and participating in building a better company, in addition to doing their regular jobs. By the same token, it is necessary for every manager leading others to be fully aware of their own responsibility for creating an environment in which talented people's potential is used to the full.

As we now have the management tools available to measure consistently over time whether bosses create such an environment, there is no longer any excuse not to meet the goal of creating circumstances under which creativity and excellence will be applied for the good of the company. We believe deeply in the power of structuring employee initiative.

While working on the foundations of our model and the definition of the operating arena, we conducted panel discussions. Participants came from international companies in different industries, were well educated and aged between 28 and 40. During discussions about what made people leave a company, elements like character, performance, integrity and support from the direct boss were mentioned time after time. Consequently, the model representing the operating arena (recall Figure 3.3) contains a section 'quality of your boss', with categories and attributes strongly linked to the above arguments:

- Winning coach.
- Influential.
- Interpersonal skills.
- Management competence.
- Trustworthy.

On the other hand, we must realize that it is not possible to take a blanket approach across the organization to the type of employee initiative environment to be created. There will be a difference from company to company, and especially from culture to culture. For example, Japan, America and Italy might differ in their ambition levels on 'employee initiative' and 'full support' because that might be partly culturally determined (Table 8.1). The CEO should check whether there are gaps within each of those different cultures. He might think, 'On a 0–100 scale I might accept a gap of a maximum of 10 for the crucial area of employee initiative' and full support', but I realize that there might be different ambition levels due to the different cultures. For example, people in some parts of the world might feel less comfortable if they have to take too much employee initiative.'

Interaction: Taking charge of communication

It is helpful if a CEO is gifted with a character that naturally radiates enthusiasm and energy. Managers throughout the organization should 'feel' the direction and the positive tension running within the company. In the creation of this energy, the corporate story is the backbone and the institutionalized dialogue is the vehicle.

Therefore, the TransCountable CEO should be as good a communicator as possible. He must realize that communication in a complex organization with thousands of people, often working all over the globe, tends to be difficult and is often very impersonal. That is why

Table 8.1 Cultural differences in ambition levels (data have not been adjusted for the fact that Japanese managers seem to score lower overall)

Average ambition levels	USA	Italy	Japan
Employee initiative	7.9	8.7	5.1
Full support	7.8	7.8	4.0

he will take advantage of new technologies and 'walk around' the organization digitally rather than physically. Here the EDC will prove its worth as an ideal vehicle to help provoke dialogue. Such dialogue also makes the CEO more visible throughout the organization, and the EDC's format will enable him to structure the 'broadcasting' (including the way the message arrives) as well as the feedback.

Take the example where a company has a division in a country far away from headquarters. The CEO's thinking can be shared with talented senior and middle managers in that division if the specific operational division agenda (emerging from that division through the results of its organizational capability scan) is combined with the strategic alignment agenda that has been formulated in the meantime. (This is the CEO's strategic agenda matched with the top priorities emerging from all divisions of the corporation.) This agenda then becomes that of the divisional general manager and, through divisional involvement, is also owned by divisional personnel. Through the transparency created in the EDC, managers deep in the organization will be able to get a feel for the relationship between the corporate and the divisional agenda. Furthermore, visibility for the company's CEO will be created without diminishing the authority of the divisional general manager. Broadcasting a video clip in the EDC of the two executives together, elaborating on their priorities, will instantly communicate the fact that they have a shared as well as an individual agenda.

The modern CEO is expected to make clear, explainable decisions based on the information received, and to make them in a timely fashion. Nevertheless, he must not be afraid to take time to reflect, and to acknowledge that he should communicate why he, and therefore the company, is following a particular path. A CEO might give orders, but people won't necessarily accept them if they can't understand why they were given.

At the same time, a CEO doesn't have to have all the answers. Part of the idea of managing by pull and push is not being afraid that, first, there might be more than one answer and, second, that it might take time to come up with the right answer. As long as managers know that structural thinking is taking place and that the CEO is leading the organization in the right direction, his subordinates will accept his authority and he will stay in control. This means that the TransCountable CEO has the ability to keep on listening to key personnel within the company, the ability to retain an open mind, and an awareness of the necessity of continually checking the alignment of the existing strategy with its execution and that the direction the company is taking is still the right one. If it isn't, he needs to make the required changes.

Making decisions is not just a rational process. Managers within any organization are realistic enough to know that coming to the right decision means using their intuition as well as analytically going through the options. Does the decision feel right? It never hurts to confront people with a human touch. This helps foster trust and ensures that other people will be less reluctant to show their human side as well. It is no coincidence that one of the 39 categories that have to be aligned for an effective operating arena is 'emotional growth'.

The first 100 days

During the first 100 days on the job, the CEO's tone of voice – virtual as well as actual – will set the standard for the rest of his tenure. This is the period during which information-gathering takes place, positions are established, and first impressions are translated into perceptions about management style, business principles and priorities. These first 100 days are often a unique opportunity to embark on the road towards TransCountability in a planned and disciplined way; communication and interaction are particularly important in this process.

For instance, the CEO of TNT, Peter Bakker, used his first 100 days to set the tone for the corporate dialogue.

TNT, a $3 billion mail and logistics company operating in 30 countries with an employee base of 140 000, appointed Peter Bakker (then aged 41) as CEO in November 2001. He had been CFO of the company for the previous five years. TNT was the result of the merger of Australian TNT and Dutch PTT Post. It was profitable, but carried a much lower multiple (price/earnings ratio) than its more aggressive peers (e.g. Federal Express).

Bakker's predecessor had the reputation of being a tough, traditional manager. Bakker was absolutely convinced that openness pays, and realized that the task ahead meant freeing himself from the shadow of this predecessor. He wanted to unlock the potential that should be in the company by challenging the available talent to get to the 'brutal facts' and create a shared agenda. Teaming up with the communications director, he set out to become a prime example of a TransCountable CEO.

The two men organized an executive session for the top 250 people in the company at the end of Bakker's first 100 days, where he planned to announce his agenda for the next couple of years. As he knew the company quite well – although from the perspective of a CFO – he had quite a firm agenda in mind, although he still wanted input and was open to possible changes. He decided to call the top 250 session 'Tough questions, straight answers'. He planned to hold executive interviews during the period before the session (physically he could achieve only a handful) and furthermore invited his top 250 people to participate in an organizational capability scan with the aim of pinpointing the company's strengths and weaknesses and discovering their agenda.

During the first weeks of January, the information was compiled, priorities formulated and the agenda defined. As one might expect, it turned out that the organization requested several changes in Bakker's agenda. He used his people's input and made some adaptations. He announced the new strategic alignment agenda to the top 250 managers during the January session and used the fact that his top people were all in one room to clarify what he meant by accountability. He stressed that accountability should not stop at the door of the CEO. He took personal accountability for projects that only he would be able to see through (because they covered the total corporation) and suggested that his divisional managers should embark on the same road towards management by pull and push. He asked them to follow through with organizational capability assessments in every country and every division.

We will learn more about TNT's and Bakker's trip towards the implementation of corporate dialogue, and the creation of an operating arena in Chapter 11 when we discuss the position of the communications director and use TNT as an illustration.

The corporate dialogue process

As we have seen, modern CEOs understand that it is their task to unlock the corporate wisdom, that they should involve their key talent, and that they need to let complexity theory work in order to allow knowledge to emerge. But, at the same time, they clearly lead and focus their companies. They open the 'black box' and move themselves into the core of the operation. They take corporate responsibility for the whole process of implementing a management style of pull and push, instead of primarily focusing on the output (the pull). They make it clear that the corporate dialogue process is not swift, but rather will take at least three to five years. It is their responsibility to lead the attitudinal *shift* so as to get people thinking in the desired manner.

Although keeping control in an increasingly complex environment is partly a question of the intention to hold a dialogue, the right measurable parameters also need to be developed and implemented. At the end of the day, measuring strategic alignment should come as naturally as measuring bottom-line performance. The CEO and his leadership team has to communicate in a language suited to the company's values and norms, a language that represents a culture of openness and integrity, of checks and balances, and not one of sweeping things under the carpet.

We have already touched on the issue of managing by example. Remember that subordinates do not so much look to their CEOs for what they say, but what they do. If the CEO does the correct things, the rest of the organization is more likely to do the same. If the CEO operates within a TransCountable mindset, is transparent about his activities and intentions, and makes it absolutely clear where his accountability lies, the chances are that he will create a transparent arena in which being accountable is considered natural. Together with his board, he is responsible for setting the strategy and taking care of the clarity of the company's intent, but he also sets the example for all the other three factors of the capacity for alignment model: how the objectives are formulated and potency is created; how the presence of enough hard and soft resources is safeguarded; and how the interaction and dialogue are carried out.

Within the EDC, the CEO creates transparency around all the aspects that he feels are relevant. He also identifies the projects for which he himself is accountable. His managers will notice that he is acting like a CEO who is embracing transparency and accountability, using his virtual CEO office to set the tone for the rest of the organization. It is much easier for a CEO to tell people in different divisions, in different business units, in different countries that they should create their own projects and foster accountability if he takes the lead and provides the example, being accessible even in an organization that employs thousands of people.

The CEO will be watched very closely to see whether or not he acts on the accountability that he has distributed and given, and whether or not he lives up to his own responsibilities. Defects in the organizational capability that come to light must be addressed; an open corporate dialogue process might turn out to constitute a threat to some people, but it is a process that cannot be stopped or reversed. If a section of leadership is negatively assessed in survey after survey, yet those managers remain in their posts, people throughout the organization will know that there are really no consequences for failure. Or, if the CEO goes out and tells the organization, 'We want to involve you, tell me what you're doing and what you want' and then doesn't' act on this information, cynicism will quickly appear in the ranks. If the corporate dialogue process isn't being led from the top, it is going to be counterproductive. Full commitment is key; otherwise, it is even in danger of collapse.

This is not a process that can be done overnight. No realistic leader will try to achieve everything at once. Instead, he will set himself the target of making his company, say, 25% more strategically aligned over the next three to five years. The *capacity for alignment index* can be used as a yardstick.

Determining the ambition level and managing gaps

What the company stands for – its ambition, values, strategic agenda, timeline and leadership – define the desired operating arena. Some companies may aspire to an arena that facilitates a great deal of *employee initiative* as well as a high level of *career ownership*, while other enterprises merely look for a solid *reputation*. The key is the alignment between the operating arena and the company's strategy. If strategy and execution are well aligned, operational effectiveness will follow.

In most cases, we have seen that the outcome of the organizational capability scan and the desired scores given by key personnel within the organization do not differ much from the status desired by the CEO. (There is an example of this with the ABN AMRO case in Appendix III.) There might be cases where the leadership aspires to an ambition level above that which in fact exists. We have also encountered a situation where the desired status of one specific category as assessed by the company's talent was adjusted downwards. Adjusting the ambition level upwards or downwards is a question of aligning the CEO's ambition and that of his people. The EDC is the ideal place to explain the defined ambition levels. Ambition levels should fit the strategic alignment agenda and therefore the company's priorities, based on its history and its future position.

But never forget that ambition levels emerging from the organizational capability scan represent the ideas of key talent within the organization and thus give evidence of the desired culture as determined by the people for the people. To overrule these levels, upwards or downwards, demands extensive dialogue, not only with the leadership team but also with key talent within the organization.

The CEO and the board

Corporate governance includes supervision by outside directors. If sustained profitability is a function of financial results and strategic alignment, then it is evident that the alignment data will be discussed with outside directors as well.

In the interests of all stakeholders, it is of pre-eminent importance that the chairman of the board and the CEO run a clear, transparent ship. There should be absolute clarity about the difference between running an organization and supervising one. Of course, the legal responsibilities of outside directors differ from country to country. In Anglo-Saxon countries, they might represent only the shareholders. There are countries in Europe, however, where the law states explicitly that directors should act in a way that represents the interests of shareholders, customers and employees alike, and a clear legal distinction is made between supervising and managing. Apart from the legal angle, however, supervising and looking after the continuity of the organization will be part of the mindset of every outside director.

There are clearly some prerequisites for a well-functioning board. In countries where there is a two-tier board, it is advisable to define specifically how the supervisory board sees its responsibility and its relationship with the management board, as well as what kind of information its members feel they need to receive in order to carry out their responsibilities.

One of the challenges of many CEOs with boards that are not tightly run is the tendency of outside directors to request specific information and then to start micro-managing on the basis of the received data. What, precisely, should be shared, apart from financial data? Sharing data related to organizational capability seems logical, as this strongly influences the company's future performance, especially when the data are published in the annual report. It may also be advisable to establish an organizational capability committee, in addition to the audit and remuneration committee.[2]

Some CEOs will share strategic alignment data with outside directors from day one. Others will prefer sharing these data only after they have become institutionalized in the company's measuring process by which budgets are guided and managers rewarded. In the latter case, pull and push management is well on its way to becoming an integral part of the company's alignment process.

Lessons learned

- People follow behaviour, not strategy. The CEO is the role model in the creation of a culture of transparency and accountability. He is the one who leads the corporate dialogue.
- We have discovered company leaders – albeit only the successful minority – who truly believe that opening up organizations through corporate dialogue will effectively drive sustainable profitability.

- Only CEOs who are financially and mentally independent have the characteristics and capabilities to manage beyond control.
- A CEO's first 100 days present the ideal opportunity to start the corporate dialogue, create support, gain authority and begin the strategic alignment process.
- It is possible for CEOs to make their mark deep inside the organization without overruling the authority of line managers responsible for individual operating areas.
- It is normal for managers from different cultures to produce different organizational capability scores. Companies and their CEOs should create an operating arena that takes these differences into account and accepts varying 'desired' and 'current' levels from different parts of the company.
- Corporate governance includes supervision by outside directors. If sustained profitability is a function of financial results and strategic alignment, it is evident that alignment data are important enough to be discussed with the outside directors as well.

9

The Chief Financial Officer
Guarding the Equation

- Keeps track of tangibles and intangibles.
- Links data and people.
- Is obsessed with the truth behind the figures.

The portfolio of responsibilities of a chief financial officer (CFO) differs from company to company, though in most cases he is a partner in strategy formulation and a guardian of the equation: *sustainable profit = financial results × strategic alignment*. By allocating financial resources, he plays a crucial role in determining the direction and speed with which different parts of the company are able to grow. He must be able to anticipate what has to become aligned and therefore he needs to have internalized the importance of organizational capabilities in realizing financial targets. In the interests of shareholders, for example, he always has an eye on the level of economic value-added. He identifies risks and protects his company against any that are unacceptable. He is responsible for making sure that the company has the financial resources available to execute its strategic agenda. It is also his responsibility to ensure that financial parameters are well defined because he is accountable for interpreting the financial data and drawing strategic and operational conclusions from them. He must also make sure that all financial personnel in his company share his convictions about the importance of organizational capabilities and operate under them.

Over the years it has become more and more evident that the CFO should possess the instinct and insight to notice what lies behind the data: he represents the conscience behind the figures.

Intent: Creating total clarity

Internal and external transparency and consistency are expected from every company. Data on strategic alignment, past and present financial figures, and rolling forecasts create a comfortable feeling about the company's past performance as well as about its future success. In this context, success ultimately means producing superior, sustainable returns on capital invested. At the end of the day, it is the CFO who makes sure that the reported numbers are not confusing and that they represent the company's real status. Transparency about what the company stands for – i.e. its intent – can be created with language, but hard figures are needed to clarify, communicate and guide: the CFO is accountable for ensuring that they do just that.

The corporate dialogue

The CFO should be an active partner in the process of aligning strategy and execution. We have already discussed the 'soft' data emerging from the organizational capability scan, but the 'hard', financial data also form an integral part of the ongoing process of dialogue, and of clarifying and obtaining input and feedback. Synthesizing these soft and hard data is a crucial skill, for which the CFO should be particularly well-suited, given the intelligence required for his position.

The annual report

The credibility of annual reports is now under fire all over the world. Ideally, the annual report should be the vehicle for transparency and accountability and give real insight into the profitability as well as the value of the enterprise. There is, of course, more than the formal 'book valuation' involved in determining the real value of a corporation. There may be undervalued assets, for example, and it is difficult to put a monetary value on elements like customer relationships, brands and patents, not to mention hidden assets such as organizational capability.

Although it is difficult for the reader of an annual report to reach a realistic valuation of the corporation, it is not as impossible as it initially appears. By looking at the current year's figures, statements about future performance, future cash flows and, if at all possible, analysing the company's organizational capability to realize future profit ambitions and industry growth, it must be possible to make a reliable assessment.

Crucial to the company's future performance is the value represented by its *corporate architecture* – what we have defined in this book as the portfolio of organizational capabilities. It is our view that this value should be identified in the accounts: investors want to know about the quality of the infrastructure. If executives are anonymously assessing a company's infrastructure and having this process verified by the auditors then, in addition to giving an insight into the strength of the organizational capability, outside stakeholders will feel increasingly comfortable about how the company looks from the inside. Even if only the measuring process is verified, in most cases readers of annual reports will be better off than they are today.

Obviously, companies might not want to share exact details of their operating arena. They might, however, want to share the fact that they allow their own people to assess their ability to execute the strategy. If this is the case, investors can assume that possible barriers to executing the strategy successfully will be exposed through the organizational capability scan, at least inside the company.

In the box below, we show an example of a verification report by PricewaterhouseCoopers. It verifies the anonymity of the data collection process and the specific details of a company's organizational capabilities.

Report from the verifiers

PRICEWATERHOUSECOOPERS

We have been asked to verify the reliability of the selected graphs and data with regards to the Corporate Architecture (Organizational Capabilities) of 'THE COMPANY': i.e. to verify the process of measurement and results of how effectively the factors of People, Structures, Systems and Culture are being organized.

Nature of verification:
'THE COMPANY' measures the state of its Corporate Architecture on a regular basis to:

- Provide performance data to managers in order to improve the effectiveness of the organization. Areas that are assessed are:
  - Quality of the Organization;
  - Culture of the Organization;
  - Image of the Organization;
  - Quality of Boss;
  - Personal Empowerment;
  - Personal Development;
  - Benefits and Rewards.
- Assure stakeholders that a process is in place to improve the effectiveness of the organization and create transparency around organizational issues,
- Assure stakeholders that an anonymous process is in place for management to address issues that require urgent attention from the Board of Management.

Scope of verification:
We have audited the reliability of the aggregated and underlying data as well as the process and methodology of the MeyerMonitor for measuring Corporate Architecture[1] (how the factors People, Structures, Systems and Culture are organized).

In our opinion:
- 'THE COMPANY' has been measuring its Corporate Architecture since the year 2000 on a regular basis.
- The measurements have taken place across the organization amongst a population identified as 'key people' (Managers, Specialists and High Potentials, i.e. Vice Presidents and higher-level managers).
- The anonymity of the participants and their assessment is guaranteed by us, and ensures honest and reliable data input.
- The graphs and data provide a true and fair view, and, together with the explanatory text, properly reflect the intentions and the aim of the company to ensure a sound Corporate Architecture.

Basis of opinion:
There are no generally accepted international standards for the reporting or verification of an organization's Corporate Architecture. We have adopted a verification approach that reflects emerging best practices, using the MeyerMonitor framework based on the best practices of a number of MeyerMonitor Participating Companies for managing and reporting a company's capability to deliver upon strategy. Therefore, we planned and carried out our work to obtain reasonable rather than absolute assurance on the reliability of this process. We believe that our work provides a reasonable basis for our opinion.

PricewaterhouseCoopers
Amsterdam

Objectives: Linking scores with capabilities

The modern CFO can play a crucial role not merely by publishing data about the company's organizational capability in the annual report, but also by helping to translate them into key performance indicators, checking them over time, 'living' them through his day-to-day work, and linking them to budgets, projects and possible investments. He can make them part of the strategic alignment agenda and link them to the company's strategic intent.

The deliverability of the budget

Any CFO is fully aware that budget figures alone are no guarantee of next year's revenues and bottom line. There is so much more that determines the final outcome: what is in the sales pipeline; how realistic are planned cost reductions; whether the forecasted new product introductions will take place and be as successful as budgeted; whether inventory targets can be reached; whether competition is allowing the company to enter a specific market; and so on and so on.

The key consideration is to look behind the figures. Budgets should be supported and adhered to throughout, and deep into, the operation. Targets must be formulated from the top down as well as from the bottom up. As we have stressed, a company managed by pull and push has a culture of dialogue, not only about the strategic alignment agenda but also about objectives and budgets resulting from this agenda. Analysing organizational capability data, division by division, will give an insight into whether targets are fully achievable. Are they accepted fully by the managerial ranks? The data that deals with how key executives regard the objectives that have been set will hold the answers. (For example, what is the true level of enthusiasm for the objectives? Are there any cultural barriers to acceptance?) And then: Can they really be attained? Clues to this will be contained in the data about capability and innovation.

The following illustration might sound familiar.

The head of a business unit simulated good results several quarters in a row by forcing bottom-line profit figures into the accounts without the board spotting what was happening. Nobody had noticed that the business unit was scraping money from every available corner during these quarters. But suddenly things started to go wrong. After the CFO investigated, it became clear what had happened.

If the company had had insight via data coming from an organizational capability scan, several warning signals might have appeared. For instance, the assessment of people in the organization on categories like shared principles and values, continuous improvement, trustworthiness of the boss, and being a responsible company would probably have shown high gaps. This might have 'blown the whistle'.

Table 9.1 Compensation based on contribution

	Corporate benchmark 2003			USA			Japan			Italy		
	DES	CUR	GAP	DES	CUR	GAP	DES	CUR	GAP	DES	CUR	GAP
Compensation based on contribution	8.2	5.7	30	8.6	5.1	29	7.1	5.2	9	8.4	5.8	22

Linking pay to results

Data from our corporate database on organizational capability indicate that both companies and many managers still desire performance-related pay as a method of rewarding people. However, the level of desirability differs from industry to industry and from company to company, from function to function and by nationality (Table 9.1).

Here again, the CFO should take responsibility for the integrity of the financial data used for the reward system, as well as for the long-term effect it might have on the company's future financial performance. The CFO is also in a perfect position to be the human resource director's sparring partner in linking rewards with organizational capability improvements.

Linking future earnings to purchase price

In acquisitions, it is common practice to apply earn-outs, under which, in addition to the agreed purchase price, an extra amount of money will be paid if the acquired company makes the budget for the following one or two years. It is not uncommon for the CFO, for the two years during which the earn-out runs, not to be allowed any supervision over the newly acquired companies. The previous owners are afraid of 'interference' and won't allow direct contact between managers from the acquiring company and executives from the acquired enterprise during the earn-out period. Their argument is that any interference might result in a lack of focus on achieving the bottom-line figure required for the earn-out. The ex-owners may even back their refusal with a threat to sue if the acquiring company does not comply.

The possible consequences are obvious. The ex-owner might put his original top executives on a very high bonus if the earn-out is achieved. At the end of the earn-out period, many of them will leave the company as rich people. The acquiring company will be left with an acquisition that has been pared to the bone, without enough experienced management left, and most likely will have difficulty delivering acceptable financial results in the forthcoming years.

Things can be handled quite differently in a company used to measuring organizational effectiveness digitally. In the situation described above, the CFO could insist that an earn-out is acceptable as long as an organizational capability scan is conducted immediately after the company has been acquired. Furthermore, the earn-out could be made not only dependent on delivering a certain bottom-line figure, but also on at least maintaining the existing quality of the company's organizational capability, as measured at the time it was acquired. Under these circumstances, the acquiring company will have a better chance of ensuring that the value of the infrastructure will not be destroyed and that sales pipelines are not totally emptied during the earn-out period.

The whole mindset of measuring strategic alignment should be reflected in the character of the CFO. Apart from his normal functional expertise, he must have a deep understanding of the corporate architecture, including the strengths and weaknesses in execution capabilities. Only then will he be able to create compelling financial objectives internally and provide outside stakeholders with the assurance that the targets can be reached.

Resources: Focus on facilitation and reality

All stakeholders, but especially the ones responsible for the company's governance, place a great deal of trust in the CFO. For example, the outside directors look to him for assurance that the company is able to fulfil its obligations and execute its strategy.

The CFO, equipped with an eye for figures plus an analytical mind, is in an ideal position to comprehend the real implications of the data under his control. For this, he certainly needs a good understanding of the status of the organizational capability, not only of the company at large but also of the various business units. This means looking at the budgets and plans of the divisions and/or business units as well as at the corporation as a whole, interpreting the organizational capability data from a financial point of view, and adding market information and any other necessary available information. The CFO must be able to see whether profit forecasts are realistic and whether the company can really execute its plans and strategies to achieve the desired results.

A deep understanding of organizational capability data will strengthen the CFO's credibility with all the company's stakeholders, internal and external. He is the person who links structural and human resources with financial resources.

Interaction: The conscience behind the data

The CFO has to represent his company in its relationship with financial institutions. Therefore, he is in a pivotal position with regard to its integrity, transparency and accountability.

Road shows and capital markets

One of the many responsibilities given to the CFO is entering capital markets for public offerings. Almost always it is the CFO who prepares the material to be presented, most likely in close collaboration with financial advisers. The company's CEO will probably chair the public offering meetings, but the CFO's credibility will be required to provide the assurance that potential investors are seeking, particularly in relation to the company's ability to generate future cash flow. Investors realize that companies might have very promising new products or services and a pipeline full of innovations, but at the end of the day executing all the plans will come down to the organizational capability. The company must have the capability to market its innovations and sell its promising new products and/or services.

Prospective investors try not to be misled by the enthusiasm of a company's chairman or CEO. After having lived through company scandals, readjustments of balance sheets and unrealized profit forecasts, these potential providers of capital are on the alert. They are aware that in most cases these problems were not caused by management failure alone; in hindsight they know that it was usually a combination of over-enthusiasm and a failure of the system to deliver the promised results. In addition, as argued in Chapter 2, investors' pressure on companies to be overly optimistic may also have been partly to blame.

Past experience, and a sense of history, may well have made investors wiser, smarter and more careful. The chances are that they require more convincing evidence of the company's capability to execute its plans than in, say, the late 1990s.

Leadership teams are dependent on the ability of hundreds of key personnel to deliver what their CEO and CFO promise during investment road shows. Having the ability to present data about the organizational capability of the last couple of years will help investors feel more comfortable about the company's potential to reach the promised targets. If the data about the status of the organizational capability are also validated by the auditors as being the anonymous assessment of the company's own key personnel, it is quite likely that this will substantially improve the level of confidence.

The next step could be for the company to promise to keep sharing these data with the investment community over time. This constitutes an overt representation of its philosophy about transparency and accountability. It also underlines the belief that sustainable profits are a function of both financial results and strategic alignment.

If the company is entering the capital markets with a specific purpose, the CFO can link the activity for which the money is required with the outcome of the organizational capability scan for the business unit designated to execute the plans. By giving insight into the organizational capability of this area of the corporation, the CFO can strengthen the confidence level of potential capital providers.

We must remember that the CFO's focus should be on assessing the financial consequences of strategic decisions. In order to do this, he has a crucial role in building the right infrastructure to capture the data – especially information needed about the company's organizational capabilities.

Keeping track of tangibles and intangibles, matching financial results with strategic alignment, linking people to data and being obsessed with the truth behind the data, will all help a CFO to be consistent, professional and active as the conscience behind the presented company data.

Lessons learned

- To identify the risks a company might face in achieving sustainable profitability, a CFO needs a solid insight into the knowledge of the company's organizational capabilities as well as its financials.
- All stakeholders expect the CFO to possess a deep understanding of what lies behind the company's figures. However, this not only includes financial data, but also the 'hard' data about 'soft' areas, i.e. data concerning organizational capabilities and strategic alignment.

- The CFO is expected to translate his analysis of the company's organizational capabilities into a valuation statement.
- The valuation of organizational capabilities should be reflected in the purchase price of acquisitions, earn-outs, budgets and reward systems.
- The ability to provide a quantified insight into the company's organizational capabilities will increase its credibility and strengthen its potential to attract external capital.
- At least one leading audit firm is offering verification services regarding organizational capabilities. Organizational capability evaluation and measurement of strategic alignment should find themselves increasingly incorporated into companies' accounts and annual reporting systems.

10

The Human Resource Director
Aligning Talent

- A transition from talent management to talent alignment.
- A shift in focus from individual talent to integrated organizational capabilities.

Although the CEO should lead the drive towards aligning strategy and execution through corporate dialogue, our experience is that in many companies it will be the human resource (HR) director who plays a leading operational role in making it all happen.

As we have stressed, managing beyond control has to become part of the company's DNA. It requires a mindset that is open, willing to be accountable, responsible for letting people be involved – in fact *requiring* them to be involved – and disciplined in following things up. All these aspects need to be reflected at all levels of the organization, a task for which the human resource director is vital.

Consider some important challenges to overcome before an effective operating arena is created and management by pull and push is fully appreciated:

- Ensuring the availability of senior managers as well as high potentials who want to operate by pull and push.
- Creating acceptance of the idea that strategic dialogue can take place outside the usual reporting lines.
- Managing a mix of people from the 'old school' and modern managers during the transformation process, while maintaining collaboration and energy in the organization.
- Consistently working on a talent-driven, meritocratic structure, based on institutionalized dialogue, without losing focus or momentum.
- Being able to give the company's key personnel maximum freedom while keeping within the strategic alignment agenda.
- Introducing and creating acceptance of a method for measuring and managing the operating arena, for whose quality individual managers will be held accountable.

It is evident that an enormous responsibility lies on the shoulders of the human resource director.

Managing by pull and push

The typical HR director will be inclined to say – and rightly so – that he has both the technical competence and the organizational responsibility to have a strong influence on many organizational capabilities in the operating arena (recall Figure 4.1), either with primary or shared responsibility.

Drilling down from the broader arena into the alignment capacity model (Figure 5.3), we find even stronger arguments for the crucial nature of this executive in creating an effective TransCountable organization. Consider the two drivers in the executive domain of the matrix and the answers to the two questions (Figure 5.4) covering these domains:

- How supportive is the organization?
- How effective is the dialogue?

In many large corporations, the HR function is slowly but steadily moving into an even more strategic position. Most of these directors now feel that they should be held accountable for the drive for organizational effectiveness and talent commitment – and in many cases they are. This means that they require a deep understanding of organizational effectiveness and the ability to help build and manage the organization so that it is aligned with the corporate strategy, creates the energy to deliver the business goals and allows talented people to realize their full potential.

If the HR director is successful in helping to achieve the process of management by pull and push, the organization will be able to support its people in achieving both their professional goals and their personal ambitions.

Intent: Giving the right people the real story

It is hard to attract, motivate and retain talented people simply by explaining that the sole purpose of the corporation is to create value for shareholders. In contrast, talented people will be motivated by the possibility of strengthening their own knowledge, becoming better professionals, being able to contribute to developing a strong, responsible company and helping to develop and market superior products and services, as well as by working for a profitable company.

When *BusinessWeek* interviewed Sam Palmisano, IBM's new CEO, he was asked how he was going to measure the company's greatness.[1] His answer neatly illustrates how many modern CEOs think:

I think about it in four or five dimensions. If you're leading the industry agenda, you should be gaining share in your core segments. In the financials, there should be real consistency in earnings. It's about cash flows and balance sheets. It's the flexibility to fund the IBM pension fund for $4 billion. Why? Because it's the right thing to do, and you can afford to do it. It's being an employer of choice. People want to be here and want to make a big difference. So it's attrition rates. And the last dimension is being viewed as a valuable *citizen. Getting people involved and using their skills to help local communities, whether that be Austin, Texas or Stuttgart.*

The challenge lies in translating these statements into HR objectives and in finding ways to measure greatness other than by financial performance alone.

Matching ambitions

An important part of the HR director's responsibilities is making sure that there is a fit or match between the company's ambition, including its organizational capability, and the ambitions of its employees.

In a company that has quantitative insights into the profiles of its talent as well as its operating arena, HR executives are able to guide this matching process carefully.

Let's take the example of Sara Lee/DE, whose board delegated to the HR director the responsibility for strengthening its entrepreneurial culture. This meant examining the corporate culture and organizational capability as well as considering individual managers by reviewing the entrepreneurial profile of the talent base.

First, a common language needed to be created. What was meant by an entrepreneurial culture?

'A company environment that stimulates professionals to make innovations to serve customers better or more cost-effectively.'

The next step was to look at the categories that correlated with the definition of entrepreneurship from the organizational capability scan. This led to what we call an 'entrepreneurial index' (see Figure 10.3 later). As Sara Lee/DE's talent base had given their desired scores (their ambition level) on the categories making up the entrepreneurial index, the HR executives could decide whether their existing talent base matched the company's ambition in respect of being entrepreneurial.

Their conclusion was that the match was not sufficiently strong. As in most corporations, it was the operating companies that recruited incoming talent, and this meant that they selected according to their own criteria, which could differ from the corporate priorities.

As a result of this matching exercise, a talent workshop was organized to which a large group of promising managers was invited. The conclusions arising from this conference were shared with the operating companies, and included a new approach to management development programmes for this category of managers.

Creating a community

Creating the right community to participate in capability scanning and in the ongoing dialogue is another important responsibility that is often put in the hands of the HR director. Frequently, it starts with a definition of talent or a description of key people. Some companies include everyone with organizational or knowledge power (the last is also a challenge to define); others go by structure, salary groups and/or the number of participants.

There are various aspects to consider, for example:

- Should you start with the top 250 and then slowly expand towards, say, 1000 or 2000 executives?
- Should the high potentials be included?

- Should you stay within the top 250 for the entire process, including the dialogue with the CEO and his leadership team, and then go down into the operating companies or divisions, which can then start their process of management by pull and push on their own terms and time schedule?
- Should the active dialogue with the company's key people be flanked with a more one-way communication process for all other employees, using the company's intranet as a vehicle?

Selecting the 'right' people for active involvement in the creation of an effective operating arena through dialogue, and creating the 'right' match between the company's intent and people's personal ambitions, are both crucial.

In several of the companies with which we have worked, the director of corporate communications also played an important role in this process. This is logical if we realize that transparency is a prerequisite for an effective, aligned operating arena – the responsibility for answering the questions 'How clear is the company's intent?' and 'How effective is the interaction?' in most cases falls within the domain of this director. If we add the fact that our corporate benchmark shows the biggest gap in transparency in communication and decision making, we see the important role that the director of corporate communications can play. We will cover the responsibilities of this director in detail in Chapter 11.

Transparent communication

Companies have found that after the CEO's initial invitation to participate in a digital assessment of the operating arena and the follow-up feedback, gaps immediately start closing in the area of transparent communication. Figure 10.1 shows the relevant section of the organizational capability scan and the illustrative case.

It is also our experience that in many companies it is the HR director who takes the initiative and starts the process of measuring and managing the operating arena – the corporate dialogue. Several possibilities are available to begin the process, which may well

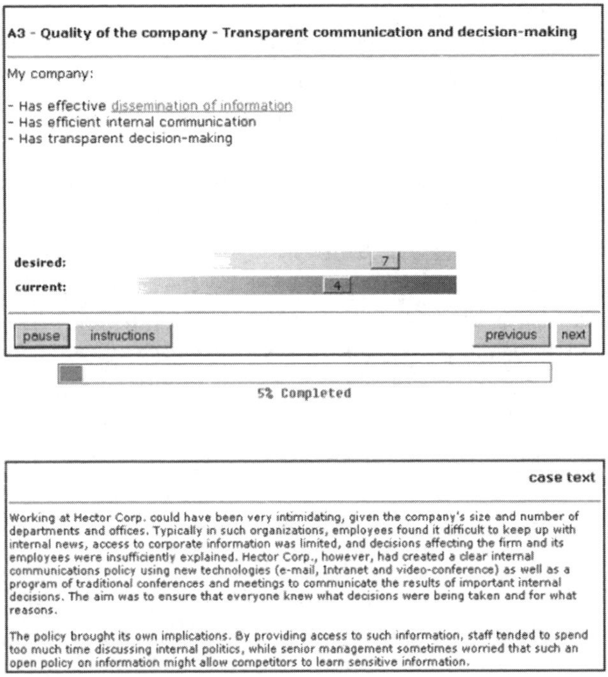

Figure 10.1 Excerpt from organizational capability scan

proceed slowly, and sometimes you just have to find an opportunity to get things going.

Here are some occasions that may inspire a person in the company to kick off the process:

- A new CEO.
- A transformation initiative.
- A merger or acquisition (including cultural integration and/or post-merger synergy).
- A corporate simplification project.

Talent alignment

The HR director can gain a deep understanding of the requirements of the talented people in his organization by analysing the data from the organizational capability scan, particularly by looking at participants' ambition levels and the gaps between their desired and current assessment of the operating arena.

Some HR directors have asked us to analyse the profile of people who have left the organization over the previous two years, in order to look for differences between this group and those who stayed. As the measurement methodology operates anonymously, we could only look at the group of people who did not appear in the most recent measurement. The results showed that between 10 and 20% of the email addresses of the previous management cycles had disappeared. The size of the group of 'leavers' did not surprise us, since figures from the US show that talented people stay in a job for an average of 3.6 years; the younger generation only stays for 2.7 years.[2]

The outcome of our analysis was quite interesting. Figure 10.2 shows the average profile for two companies (which we combined), comparing leavers to stayers. As you can see, there is a significantly different profile.

This kind of hard data, in combination with exit interviews, should help the HR director to gain a deeper understanding of how to match talent more closely with the firm's operating arena. Next to being strategically aligned, one of the best predictors of a company's overall excellence is its ability to attract, motivate and retain talented people.

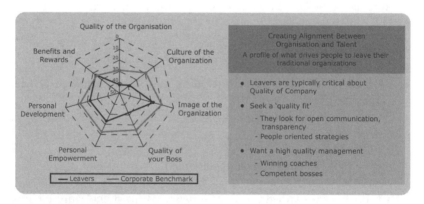

Figure 10.2 Analysis of stayers and leavers for two companies

Retaining the best people

In order to strengthen its management base, Warner Lambert, a large multinational pharmaceutical company[3], wanted to attract the best candidates from the best business schools, both in the US and abroad. To make sure that it could hire these talented young people, it decided to offer them a salary of 25% above the market rate.

Within the company's corporate HR department, a manager was appointed to coordinate these new recruits, to follow their progress and take responsibility for this program. After joining the company these young people were sent out around the world and put into different positions in operating companies.

We conducted an organizational capability scan within this organization among 600 managers worldwide. The 'High Professionals' (HiPros) could be identified as a group. The results were quite interesting when we looked at the differences between HiPros' scores and total company results. It was especially interesting to look at both the desired and current scores in some of the categories (Table 10.1).

The conclusion was clear: the corporation had hired potentially great managers who after a short period already showed high gaps between 'desired' and 'current' on attributes connected with initiative. Although they were paid well, it appeared they had been placed in a position where they could not use their potential as much as they wanted. This example illustrates the advantage of hard data in offering full transparency, which should result in managerial accountability for creating a supportive organization (the southeast quadrant of the capacity for alignment model).

Warner Lambert needed to decide who should be held accountable for retaining the 'HiPros' group and what action could be taken to create a challenging environment in which they could exercise their initiative.

Table 10.1 'HiPros' versus company total (the research was done before the company was acquired by Pfizer)

	Warner Lambert Total			Warner Lambert HiPro's		
	DES	CUR	GAP	DES	CUR	GAP
High level Strategy Participation	8.0	5.8	20	8.5	5.5	52
Freedom to act	8.4	6.4	8	8.7	6.1	31
Employee value creation	7.9	5.4	27	8.4	4.9	37
Meritocracy	8.0	5.4	27	8.2	5.0	41
Exposure to the unfamiliar	7.3	5.8	7	7.7	4.6	30

New recruits need to flow through an organization in a way that enables them to support existing line management without losing their commitment and enthusiasm. In particular, HR directors in charge of high potentials in large organizations will understand the advantage of keeping track of their talented personnel while they are in different countries and under the responsibility of different line managers with different management styles. The power of hard data will give these HR directors an edge by enabling them to follow these people, supporting, developing and, last but not least, retaining them for the well-being of both the corporation and those talented individuals themselves.

The matching process and recruitment

A well-prepared candidate for a job who, through an organizational capability scan, has made an accurate self-analysis to assess what he or she requires, will be pleasantly surprised to find a company that has a detailed scan of its organization available for both the total corporation and different countries and business units. Just consider a graduating MBA student bringing his desired operating arena assessment into the recruitment process and comparing it with two business units of a specific multinational company, as illustrated in Table 10.2.[4]

Comparing the profile of the MBA graduate with the expected operating arena in the different business units gives a good indication

Table 10.2 Operating arenas compared

	New recruit			Business Unit A			Business Unit B		
	DES	CUR	GAP	DES	CUR	GAP	DES	CUR	GAP
Transparent communication & decision making	9.0	6.1	45	9.2	7.9	5	8.1	5.2	27
Result and output driven	8.4	6.3	40	8.3	6.9	6	7.9	4.8	36
Professional development	8.7	6.8	24	8.9	6.5	22	8.3	4.6	51
Emotional and creative growth	8.0	6.3	21	8.6	7.1	5	7.8	5.2	25
Leadership competence	8.3	7.0	14	8.3	6.9	3	7.8	6.0	15

of where the best match lies. (The current score was the situation in the candidate's job before taking an MBA, and the desired score the type of corporate environment the candidate wanted.) Another possibility would be for the company to put its organizational capability scan on its website. Candidates could fill in their ambition level (what they are looking for) and answer the questions under 'current' in relation to their existing job. Based on the outcome, a company could have candidates interviewed by a business unit that closely matches their desired organizational profile.

The matching process and executive placement

The organizational capability scan can also be used to great effect within the organization. Take a hypothetical division in a particular country. This division has problems – financial, management and executional – that show up on the scan. A certain picture of what people are looking for in their division emerges out of the data, in relation to culture as well as desired leadership.

Based on past bottom-line performance and the negative outcome of the scan, the management board decides to ask the HR director to replace the general manager in question. The HR director is able to create the profile for a suitable replacement based on what people are asking for in that part of the world, as well as what the structure requires. There may be a division operating in a nearby country in the same geographic region where the same management style might be applicable and where the results of the organizational capability scan show an excellent boss, good results and a profile that is very close to

Table 10.3 Two divisions compared

Assessment Profile Boss & Culture	Division in trouble			Division in succes		
	DES	CUR	GAP	DES	CUR	GAP
Winning coach	8.5	3.0	87	8.7	7.9	0
Interpersonal skils	8.2	4.3	54	8.5	7.9	0
Direct & action oriented	8.4	4.7	58	8.3	6.7	12
Meritocracy	8.8	5.5	41	8.7	6.2	19

the desired aspects for the problematic country. Table 10.3 shows the difference between assessment scans done in two divisions of a sample company within the same geographic region.

If he decided to replace the general manager of the division in the problem country with the one from the division in the successful country, interpreting the data from the organizational capability scan would give the HR director a great deal of useful information.

Objectives: Fighting for meritocracy

In an open, meritocratic company, managers should be rewarded for strengthening their corporate or business operating arena, as well as for their bottom-line performance. There is a fine line to be walked in matching the value of experience, loyalty and even seniority with promotions based on meritocracy, often within a strong culture of performance-based payment.

Overall, meritocracy has to do with having the right mindset and being able to quantify objectives, including quantifying the quality of the operating arena.

Marketing and finance executives have the advantage of not having to convince anybody that their work is linked to today's and tomorrow's bottom-line performance. They can support their arguments with hard data, comparing yesterday's situation with today's and with the budget. From there, it is relatively easy to reach a forecast for tomorrow. Marketing people have learned how to translate customers' perceptions of price, quality and service into hard facts, and have had the experience of linking research data on price and quality image (perception) directly with sales and then bottom-line performance.

In a typical management board meeting, the finance director makes a case for an increase in the growth margin. This is necessary because it appears that the company will not make its budgeted profit forecast. The marketing director warns that if price increases are not followed by the competition, they will have a negative influence on the price image that customers have of the company's product range. He argues that the price image will worsen, which will be followed in the next quarter by a loss of market share. In the end, the increase in the growth margin might be outweighed by the loss of sales.

The decision in the boardroom might be to raise some prices carefully, then continue doing market research in order to monitor the customer's price perception of the company's products, especially in comparison with competitors. The moment the price image decreases by more than a particular percentage, the board should meet again and decide on the next steps.

The full board is used to this line of thinking and is convinced of the importance of 'customer value' data, realizing that it has an impact on sales. The marketing executive in question might in the end be asked to cut some costs from his budget because of concerns over the profit forecast.

Now let's turn to the HR director. Intellectually, his colleagues realize that innovation is a key driver for new products and new services, that a well-structured organization is a key driver for effectiveness and efficiency, and that all this can be summarized under the heading of operating arena. They all agree with the HR director that in the long run investment in strengthening organizational effectiveness will have a positive effect on bottom-line performance. They also follow his arguments that if managers neglect all these aspects, it will destroy value. But since this intellectual capital, this structural value, will not show up in any financial statements, the discussion about a necessary budget cut in the HR section often ends up being general, qualitative and 'as soft as butter'.

The finance director who approached the marketing director about cost reductions now starts the same discussion with the HR director and begins making suggestions about budget cuts: skip the next management event, postpone the introduction of the new benefits and reward system, and/or reduce the planned advertising campaign that had been considered necessary to make the company a more attractive employer. In this case, it is much more difficult to come up with hard data to monitor a change in employees' perception of their ability to execute the company's strategy (the weakening of the operating arena). Nevertheless, it is exactly this last aspect that has a strong influence on future years' bottom-line performance.

Until quite recently, HR directors faced problems in coming up with hard data that were consistent over time. Apart from the fact that reports on organizational capability were often difficult to read, they were not comparable with earlier reports and were often published too late to be effective. Traditionally, most data were collected several months before the report was presented at a management board meeting, and so were frequently dismissed with the argument that matters had changed in the meantime.

Let's compare these two situations: the marketing director versus the HR director. We can almost predict the outcome of the cost-cutting management team meeting: like marketing, HR has to cut its budget, but the discussion probably takes a different angle. The HR director will most likely be asked to cut costs and then closely monitor reactions within the organization; possibly he will be asked not to talk too much about it; and if key talent leave within the next six months he should keep the board informed about their reasons. His colleagues will suggest that if, in six months, he feels it necessary, he should put the issue back on the agenda. They will argue that the HR director should realize that competitors are also in a difficult financial position because of market circumstances, and therefore they will also probably cut back on all kinds of 'extras'. Thus, in the board's view, the company's competitive position will not really worsen – it might just make this year's forecast. If things go better next year, board members promise, we can spend the money and will execute all the planned HR projects.

The moral of this story is that until strategic alignment is consistently measured over time and organizational capability is translated into key performance indicators and made part of reward systems, the HR director will find it difficult to operate on an equal footing with his fellow senior executives.

Resources: Being committed to engagement

A key question in the process of engaging people is: 'How supportive is the organization?' Certainly, engagement has to do with the individual, but also crucial are the circumstances an organization creates that make engagement possible.

As the Warner Lambert example illustrated, attracting brilliant people by allocating extra budget to human resources is one thing, but keeping them engaged is a wholly different matter. The creation of engagement can be illustrated using the earlier example of Sara Lee/DE, which wanted to create a more entrepreneurial culture. The company wanted talent that had strong entrepreneurial ambitions, but also appreciated that the organization needed to be supportive and allow talent to be entrepreneurial.

For Sara Lee/DE, 14 categories from the organizational capability scan covering the company's definition of an entrepreneurial operating arena were selected and put into a 'basket'. An *entrepreneurial tracking index* based on the categories below could then be formulated. The basket contained:

Quality of company
- Result and output driven.
- Reinvent for growth.
- Customer value creation.

Culture of company
- Direct and action oriented.
- Employee initiative.
- Meritocracy.
- Adaptive and open to change.

Image of company
- Dynamic industry player.

Quality of boss
- Winning coach.
- Influential.

Personal empowerment
- Freedom to act.
- Maximum challenge.
- People mobilization.

Personal development
- Exposure to the unfamiliar.

How well the operating arena is aligned to accommodate entrepreneurship can be captured through an entrepreneurial gap index:
- *The corporate or business entrepreneurial gap index*: the level of entrepreneurial improvement potential in the operating arena.
- *The corporate or business entrepreneurial ambition index*: the ambition level of the entrepreneurial aspects in the operating arena.
- *The corporate or business entrepreneurial index*: the strength of the entrepreneurial aspects in the operating arena.

First, by looking at the data in the different indices, the organization can get a solid idea of the current and desired level as well as the general status of its potential to support its managers in being entrepreneurial.

In order to go a step deeper in the analysis, the categories can be compared between varying groups of managers and business units. Figure 10.3 shows that individual business units scored differently on the entrepreneurial tracking index. The company data show that the Sara Lee/DE's operating arena has various subcultures, at least in the area of entrepreneurship. This is probably the case in many companies, but it exemplifies the great power that comes from hard data.

The different entrepreneurial indices were also compared for the total Sara Lee group with data from other fast-moving consumer goods (FMCG) companies (Figure 10.4). This shows where the 'best-in-class' company is located (northeast corner with a gap of 10) and the worst company (southwest corner with a gap of 29).

In order to understand in greater detail the ambition levels of young talented managers, Sara Lee held a three-day strategy meeting involving young managers and the board of management. Part of the programme was devoted to entrepreneurship. To prepare for this workshop, additional online research was carried out to identify the specific challenges for entrepreneurship at the company.

Some interesting observations came to light in the resulting indices. There was sufficient opportunity to work on entrepreneurial projects, and quite a few entrepreneurial people available. However, according to this talented group, there were some specific barriers to strengthening the entrepreneurial culture. The managers at the strategy meeting concluded the following:

- The company had slightly too much focus on short-term rather than long-term results. Talented people found that they had no time to spend on entrepreneurial projects.
- There should be more benefits for spending time on entrepreneurial ideas.
- Bureaucracy, which slows down decision making, should be cut back.
- There should be more effective cross-functional collaboration.
- Getting more support from senior management was the most important pre-condition for making entre-preneurship work.
- Tolerance of mistakes and a willingness to take risks should be increased.
- There was a need to take more time to understand the details of projects.

During the three-day session, the Board and the young managers discussed these conclusions and defined the resulting action items.

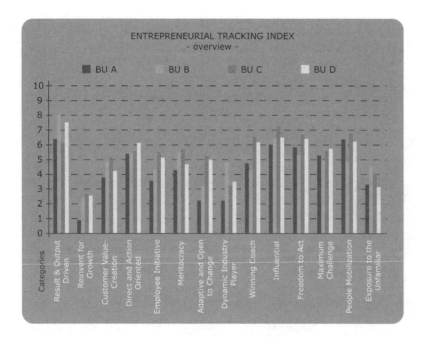

Figure 10.3 Entrepreneurial tracking indexes for different business units

Improving organizational capabilities

It is probably the HR director who will be asked to support line management in making sure that divisions and business units measure organizational capability, define projects and close gaps. It is our experience that during the first years of creating a successful corporate dialogue by measuring, matching and managing, it is HR directors who work best with the data. It is they who notice the gaps widening or closing.

It is also our experience that if a situation has deteriorated, it is the HR director who will contact the appropriate division or business unit manager and ask for possible causes. He is often the one who, together with the relevant manager, can look for a potentially simple explanation. The confidence created by such hands-on involvement

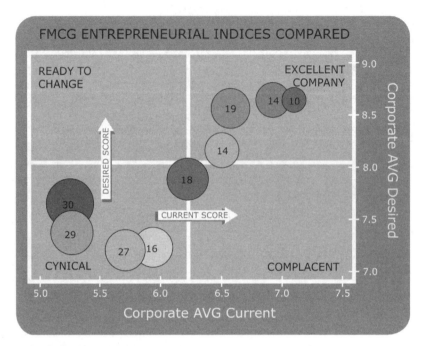

Figure 10.4 FMCG companies compared

will put him in an ideal position of trust, support and, of course, organizational power.

Interaction: Fighting for openness

Next to the company's CEO, it should be the HR director who continually pushes for openness and leads by example. People will note whether transparency, involvement and dialogue come as naturally to his department as to the company as a whole. This transparency not only covers openness about administrative and career information (where many of the companies we examined are now doing extremely well), but also the total HR function and its relationship with line management.

Leading by example

To illustrate how a modern HR director can lead by example, we now consider the actual case of a newly appointed HR director at Heineken.

Table 10.4 Sample organizational capabilities for Heineken

	Heineken		
	DES	CUR	GAP
A solid image	8.6	8.0	0
Meritocracy	8.4	5.8	27
Compensation based on contribution	8.3	5.2	34
Full support	8.5	6.4	11
Continious improvement	8.6	6.2	23
Transparent communication & decision making	8.6	5.3	42

The challenge was to place the HR department firmly on the map within a 'line and operations' driven company. At Heineken, the brand and brewing were king: it was 'an institution in marble'. Within such a company, what is the role of HR in talent alignment and organizational effectiveness? Is there actually such a role at all, and if so, who bears the accountability? Does that stay with line management, or should it be shared? From Table 10.4, we can see that there were clearly some HR challenges in the company's culture (e.g. in meritocracy) as well as rewards system gaps (e.g. in contribution-based payment).

Thony Ruys, the company's newly-appointed CEO, was determined to address these issues, particularly in view of the company's recently announced new focus for the coming years: 'Taking Heineken to the Next Level'. Specifically, the three themes making up that new focus would all deeply involve HR:

- 'Shape the business' (HR link) Support organizational effectiveness.
- 'Increase performance' (HR link) Promote for performance.
- 'Build a more challenging and supportive culture' (HR link) Inspire people to take initiative and reward support.

Ruys realized the importance of improving transparency around the company's intent as well as establishing clear accountability for organizational effectiveness. He was also convinced that talent engagement was vital to the company's future. Clarity about the positioning of the HR function would be crucial in the success of his 'next-level' scenario. Why not lead by example?

The newly-appointed HR director had the task of formulating objectives for her own area of expertise. She intended to create accountability for her people at corporate level, as well as for HR managers in operating companies, who reported to powerful line managers and were only functionally accountable to her. The question was how to involve the line in defining responsibilities, and what method to use.

About 300 managers – both line and staff, HR and others, senior as well as junior executives – were asked to give their assessment of the current and desired performance of the HR function. The same measuring methodology was used here as in the earlier organizational capability scan, i.e. desired, current and gap scores were generated.

The following conclusions were drawn from the research:

- Heineken has a high requirement for HR support services. Therefore, executives, particularly the management board and corporate directors, are generally critical of HR's performance.
- Heineken's managers want corporate HR to focus mainly on improving traditional HR issues. They don't want HR to be so involved in redefining strategy, but do want it to

foster cultural change initiatives, improve employee commitment and competencies, and ensure the effectiveness of HR processes.
- The main role of corporate HR should be to disseminate knowledge and improve the quality of processes. It should focus on providing tools to do this and on sharing best practice.

Three weeks later these results were taken into a three-day workshop with HR staff. They were used to obtain a clear definition of the responsibilities of the HR function, both corporate and within the operating companies. For the HR director, this not only provided the possibility of creating clarity among her own personnel, but also meant that she could emphasize the importance of regional operational people supporting their line managers to help them increase organizational effectiveness. She found this a necessary step, as she realized that creating a strong operating arena (through a pull and push management style and the creation of shared agendas) throughout Heineken would be an important challenge for HR.

There was particular discussion of HR's level of responsibility for organizational effectiveness. Would it only provide tools and methodologies, or should HR take the lead and force their implementation? It was agreed that corporate HR would play a deciding role in measuring organizational capability. Corporate as well as divisional HR would share best practices and advise line management about closing gaps in areas where Heineken's new strategic agenda and execution were not aligned. This opportunity enabled HR to have a more strategic impact within the firm.

To this end, the HR director presented her staff with her HR vision, based on Heineken's updated strategic priorities. At the conference, the corporate- and operating-level HR executives discussed the priorities in groups, indicating what they expected from headquarters as well as deciding on their own focus.

> Equally important was the fact that almost 300 key people from the company as a whole had been involved in determining the accountability of the HR function. From that moment on, the new HR director could start executing her agenda, which was shared with and owned by the company.

The HR director has to be a key player in managing a company's strategic alignment. In many cases, he will play a pivotal role in setting up the process, which measures the status of the operational arena. Furthermore, he will lead and track many of the strategic alignment improvement projects. Being responsible for the optimal alignment of both existing and incoming talent with the operating arena will make him a key strategic partner in the process of management beyond control.

Lessons learned

- The HR director can now access hard data on organizational capabilities, and this puts him in a good position strategically. The knowledge enables him to support both the strategic and talent alignment processes.
- The HR director is a key player in the corporate dialogue, because he usually selects and creates the specific community of key executives involved in the alignment process.
- Aligning talent and organizations means making the operating arena fit the expectations of the talented people tasked with executing strategy. Moreover, it involves fully engaging these talented people. One has to do with structure, the other with people, but both are measurable over time.
- By using organizational capability data, the HR director is able to appoint and replace the appropriate people, formulate recruitment profiles and provide insights as to why people have left the organization.

- Organizational capability data make it possible to monitor over time the progression through the company of any given pool of talented future leaders.
- Strategic alignment without meritocracy is impossible, but hard data are necessary if the organization wants to reward on merit. The HR director plays a crucial part in establishing such a system by using consistent data about personal performance and capability over time.
- The degree of entrepreneurial spirit and capability can be measured through an entrepreneurial gap index. This determines the level of entrepreneurial ambition and improvement potential in the operating arena.
- *Managing beyond control* implies managing capabilities. The HR contribution to fostering leadership beyond control is strengthened by creating transparency and accountability through the digital dialogue process around HR capabilities between line management and the HR function.

11

The Communications Director
The coherent, consistent storyline

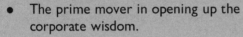

- Spearheads a move from informing and explaining to involving and challenging.
- The prime mover in opening up the corporate wisdom.

intent   objectives

operating
arena

interaction   resources

In the commercial sense, corporate communications is a combination of listening and interacting, with the purpose of engaging company stakeholders in helping the company build and maintain success. The communications director has to take into account both internal and external stakeholders. Companies are not separated from their environment; obviously, they have a great deal of interaction with external stakeholders such as shareholders, customers, local communities, regulators and politicians.

To complicate matters, the traditional constellation that shows stakeholders as distinct groupings, each an independent circle defending its own interests, is now outdated. Today, these groupings are blurring: employees are increasingly shareholders and often customers; other companies can be partners at one time and competitors at another; local communities can raise concern about the environmental impact of an industrial facility while simultaneously being dependent on it for employment. Today's stakeholder maps are best illustrated as a series of overlapping circles, forming *ad hoc* coalitions on specific issues.

The increasing role of outsourcing and partnering has also made the boundaries of the firm itself less rigid. As the transaction costs in the economy decline, so does the need for vertical integration. Most companies outsource elements of services like IT, HR or finance; many buy manufacturing capacity and use multiple distribution channels. Their resulting focus on ever-narrower slices of the value chain means that they need to form long-term and dependable strategic partnerships.

When companies collaborate, the traditional command-and-control paradigm becomes increasingly ineffective. Managing by pull and push, setting common goals and being accountable for meeting them, as well as being transparent about the drivers of costs – in essence, being TransCountable – are all key to successful partnerships.

Broadening the dialogue to include society

So what is the impact of blurring corporate boundaries? When external entities are fulfilling vital roles for the organization and stakeholder roles overlap, communication and therefore transparency and accountability need to extend to this wider set of players. And when a company is externally transparent and accountable, naturally, people will ask about its purpose and its contribution to society. These questions are likely to come from nongovernmental organizations (NGOs), local communities and governments, and also from employees, and it is generally the communications director who has to deal with them.

There is an additional benefit to making the company accountable to a wider set of stakeholders: by creating a culture of open dialogue, you create a virtuous circle of reinforcement that ultimately improves organizational capability.

The internal corporate dialogue

We will now focus on a specific example – that of TNT – to illustrate the role of the communications director as a key operator in the internal corporate dialogue. As we will see, this internal dialogue demonstrates the contribution of connections to external stakeholders, through the different sustainable development initiatives in which TNT is engaged.

The communications director is always strongly dependent on the CEO. If he is in the fortunate situation of reporting to a leader who is convinced that transparency pays, he can play a crucial role in the alignment process, i.e. in the corporate dialogue. It is our experience that the person in this position can become the right hand and key sparring partner of the CEO. Certainly, this is what we found at TNT, which also provides an excellent example of implementing the management beyond control process.

Intent: Making sense of strategy
through interaction

In Chapter 8, we described CEO Peter Bakker's first 100 days. During this period, he and communications director Peter van Minderhout began creating operational push by an active process of dialogue. Their goal was to create absolute clarity about the direction the company was taking and make sure that the aim of the strategy was well understood.

Bakker's first step as CEO was to redefine the company's strategic priorities and make a serious attempt to create ownership around them. As mentioned earlier, he was already familiar with TNT having previously been CFO, so he started out with a clear idea about what the company should stand for and its possible strategy. He had a personal agenda as well as some specific ideas about management and how a CEO should operate. In his view, strategy is not difficult, should not be kept secret, and is not only for big shots within the company. He wanted to differentiate TNT from other players in the industry through three specific corporate values: sustainability, responsibility and transparency.

Bakker believes that a CEO should be visible at the middle of his company where the direction and sometimes the priorities of the strategy, as well as the quality of its execution, can be continuously challenged. This does not mean holding a permanent discussion that bypasses normal reporting lines: on the contrary, to keep the company performing well, day-to-day reporting lines should be maintained, if only because budgets have to be followed and supervisors have to be certain that their instructions are executed. On the other hand, managers should feel free to try alternatives and be on the lookout for improvements, within a framework that combines strategic priorities and corporate values. Ultimately, this leads towards the strategic alignment agenda, which should be shared and owned throughout the company.

Bakker tried to achieve this ownership through a structured, multi-year process of talent involvement. At the start of his tenure as CEO in October 2001, he invited a group of key executives and talent, called respectively the Top 200 and the Mirror Board, to assess the company's organizational capabilities. This was a first step towards the creation of a shared list of company priorities, and the first step towards management by strategic pull and organizational push. The idea was to let this happen during the company's annual senior management meeting (ASMM), which took place in January each year.

In preparation for the ASMM of 2002, a series of questions and strategic dilemmas was digitally distributed to the executives participating in the conference and to a group of upcoming talent. This last group would also function as a control group to create a balanced view about the perceived organizational capabilities.

It was the communication director's task to manage not only the meeting but also the organizational capability scan that was to precede the ASMM. The first step was deciding exactly whom to involve, and how to word the formal Internet invitation to assess the company.

The conference was themed 'Tough Questions – Straight Answers'. It was the start of a new era in which a modern CEO,

Table 11.1 Initial reactions to TNT's organizational capability scan

Dear Peter,
Good to notice that our new director desires to get in touch with large groups of
TPG employees, even though he is a long distance away from many of them.
Especially the internal use of internet communication can help us use the external
possibilities in this area to the fullest.

So you can count on my support.

Dear Peter,
Thank you very much for your openness and
Interest in wanting to know the
'heartbeat' of our organization.
I am gratified to share the feedback honestly
and constructively.
With Best Regards,

Thanks Peter,

I like this approach very much!

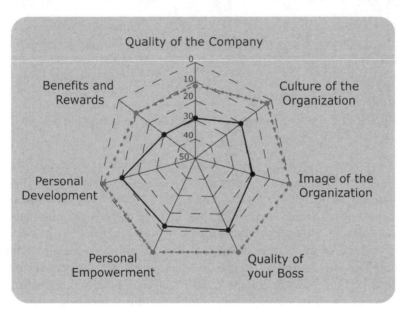

Figure 11.1 Spider diagram for TNT – the dotted line shows, for each section, best in class from the full corporate benchmark

paired with a powerful communications director, embarked the company on a dialogue-driven adventure.

The reactions that Peter Bakker had received in November 2001 from the executives invited to participate in the preliminary organizational capability scan had been very encouraging (Table

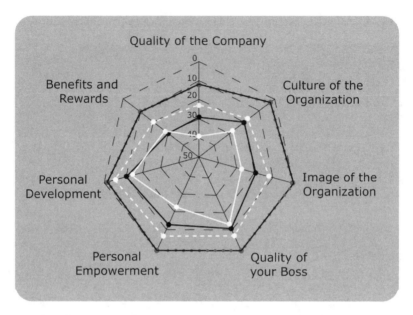

Figure 11.2 Spider diagram for TNT, showing different divisions

11.1). They were also quite revealing. As described above, Bakker had formulated several strategic priorities on which he and the company were to concentrate. Analysing the data from the scan, he knew that he had to reprioritize. We can see the areas of alignment and misalignment from the spider diagram in Figure 11.1. Some aspects concerning the quality of the company were open for improvement, as well as several areas in the section on benefits and rewards. The organization was actually telling Bakker to concentrate first on setting things right within the company, namely strengthening quality aspects and addressing benefits and rewards issues.

The spider diagram in Figure 11.2 shows a wide range in the level of alignment of organizational capabilities from division to division. All the divisions needed to improve in order to become 'future proof'; all had some distance to go to become best in class. Communication, in this case through digital dialogue, had indeed brought out the brutal facts.

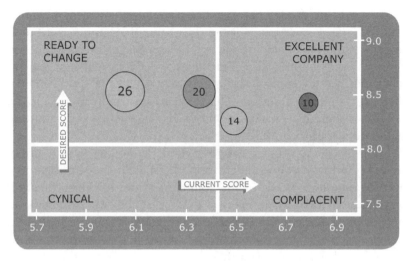

Figure 11.3 Divisional analysis from TNT organizational capability scan

Figure 11.3 shows the three divisions as well as the 'best in class' mark (gap of 10). The vertical and horizontal axes represent the ambition and current levels respectively, and the size of the bubble represents the gaps.

Bakker presented the findings himself at the ASMM and asked his divisional managers to deepen their understanding of the issues for each division during 2002. Immediately, he took personal accountability for one operational issue emerging from the findings and added that to the company's priorities: the reward system.

During the remainder of 2002, the organizational capability scan was repeated by two of the three divisional vice-presidents. The purpose was to drill down on the issues, involve more people and therefore commit more managers to the implementation of shared strategic priorities. The HR department undertook specific initiatives to develop benefits and rewards solutions.

The next phase started in late 2002. The idea was to further strengthen clarity around the company's intent and move from a list of priorities, as defined during Bakker and Van Minderhout's first ASMM, towards a more formal shared strategic alignment agenda.

Bakker and van Minderhout formulated a set of six relevant dilemmas and two open questions (Table 11.2) in order to deepen their understanding about ambition levels, the key managers' confidence in the company's future and real attitudes about its social engagement. They decided to expand the group of participants in the digital dialogue from 450 to 1300. This served as an indication that the board was committed to continuing the management style of strategic pull and operational push.

Internal communications were pivotal in moving from a list of shared priorities towards the creation of a shared strategic alignment agenda. The importance of the communications director's function was more evident than ever. For Bakker and van Minderhout, organizing the survey in late 2002 and then acting on it was an indication that transparency and accountability were to be taken seriously. Also, it made clear that the ability to face the truth was an important leadership quality in TNT's culture.

Interaction: Managing the ecosystem of dialogue

The strategic alignment agenda can be brought alive through various methods. In the case of TNT, it was the communications director who proposed for the CEO and the company six unusual, but highly effective, steps:

- Personally demonstrating the desired confrontational behaviour by conducting a risky personal interview with the BBC.
- Embarking on a global tour.
- Opening a virtual CEO office.
- Designing people-based key performance indicators (KPIs) for management.
- Measuring engagement on a global scale.
- Chat sessions.

Interview with the BBC: Step 1 saw the razor-sharp BBC reporter Tim Sebastian, known throughout most of Europe for his television programme *Hard Talk*, interviewing – or rather interrogating – Peter

Table 11.2 TNT issues to be discussed

Growth	My Division should grow through continuing mergers and acquisitions.	VS	My Division should grow organically by focusing on existing business.
Financial Performance	Earnings improvements in my Division should come from greater efficiency and control.	VS	Earnings improvements in my Division should come from investments in innovative projects.
People management	It is important that TPG values people only if they continue to perform and deliver results.	VS	It is important that TPG values people for their loyalty and contribution over-time.
Industry Leadership	To be a leader in the industry my Division does all the right things.	VS	To be a leader in the industry my Division should change its strategy significantly.
Our Market Position	It is important that my Division is aggressive in attracting new clients and winning new markets.	VS	It is important that my Division retains current clients and builds upon existing relationships.
Organizational Effectiveness	My division should increase organizational effectiveness by incremental improvements.	VS	My division should increase organizational effectiveness by rethinking our processes.

Table 11.3 Sample questions from senior management group

Yes/No question 1	Say, TPG shares are below 18 euro a share and you have some excess funds, would you buy?
Yes/No question 2	Do you believe our partnership with the World Food Programme will be beneficial to TPG?

Bakker. The tough questions and answers were taped and shown during the ASMM in January 2003. These clearly highlighted the difficult choices that CEOs face. The reaction from the audience (almost 300 executives) was warm and enthusiastic.

The global tour: Step 2 involved Bakker and van Minderhout embarking upon a four-month journey after the ASMM called the 'Cascade', during which they met with roughly 1500 TNT executives at company outposts as far apart as Jacksonville, Birmingham, Paris, Milan, Amsterdam, Singapore, Tokyo and Sydney. This represented a considerable investment of time and energy in the fostering of local interaction and dialogue. Local management hosted these sessions, and invited their staff. Professional videos and background materials supported them and ensured consistency of the message across the globe. All events were digitally supported by a dedicated website, through which the participants were encouraged to deliver tough questions from six different viewpoints: client, employee, shareholder, analyst, competitor, and member of society. Van Minderhout's office then grouped these questions into themes, for presentation back to the local executives shortly before he and Bakker arrived for a visit. Once face-to-face with local managers, the company's two top men deliberately kept formal presentations to a minimum, since their desired focus was on interaction – questions asked and answers given, by both local and visiting personnel.

The dialogue turned out to be confrontational although, reflecting the various cultures, there was a different tone in different parts of the world. During these sessions, Bakker personally presented the results of the dilemmas and open questions. He talked about his responsibility, his accountability, the role of talent and the importance of organizational effectiveness. He invited interaction and promised further dialogue, and tasked Van Minderhout with making this commitment happen.

Everywhere these two executives travelled, the company's new programme for supporting sustainable development – called the 'Moving the World Initiative' – was much-discussed. It had been developed in affiliation with the UN World Food Programme, but had initially started in response to the demand coming from TNT's managerial ranks for an initiative to combine the company's logistical competence with social responsibility.

The virtual CEO office: During the global Cascade, the formal decision was made to institutionalize the dialogue between the CEO and a select group of the company's key executives in a virtual CEO office, an *executive dialogue centre* (Step 3). Once again, the importance of the communications director stood out as he took personal responsibility for getting this institutionalized dialogue started. This involved leveraging the CEO's time by permanently placing him at the middle of the company via the virtual CEO office.

During the summer and autumn of 2003, van Minderhout's staff analysed the items of the CEO's agenda and created presentations to expound and support them. The challenge of communicating abstract concepts such as integrity to 60 different countries with different cultures was considerable, and it didn't help that the target audience had expanded in the meantime from the original 1500 to roughly 2500 managers. To meet the challenge, staff made use of audio and video resources in addition to print, to drive home the importance of those agenda items for attaining sustainable success for the company.

People-Based KPIs: Step 4 occurred during the summer of 2003, when human resource initiatives were aligned with the new style of pull and push. A human resources taskforce was created to work on a people-based management strategy. The team designed three 'people accountability' KPIs – Commitment and Engagement, Performance Management and Talent Management – which were introduced in 2004.

Measuring Engagement: Step 5 was the logical result of Bakker and van Minderhout witnessing the effect that the new company internal communication had on employee engagement. The new TNT10 Engagement initiative then extended the new internal communication lines beyond the original 2500 managers to an even-broader internal audience.

Chat Sessions: the final step in the process was the start of pre-scheduled 'chat' sessions on various important topics, conducted via the executive dialogue centre. For instance, at the end of 2003, 150 managers all over the world were discussing online TNT's expansion strategy in China. This session was followed in early 2004 with another 'chat' about company values.

Objectives: Enabling individual agendas to be aligned with the strategic alignment agenda

The communications director also plays a pivotal role in creating a pull and push mindset throughout the company. Managers, often speaking many different languages, are working everyday on their daily tasks deep inside large multinational corporations. These tasks are most likely based on the agendas set by their division, business unit and direct superior. Individual managers then create their own *implicit* agenda, covering how they see the situation and what is necessary to get things done. We need to merge *individuals'* implicit agendas with the explicit priorities, i.e. objectives, formulated by the company as a whole. Such common objectives can then be 'brought alive' to everyone, not only by assigning key performance indicators, but also by clearly linking these objectives to what the company stands for – the corporate story – of which the communications director is the guardian.

Resources: Infrastructure as an enabler for consistency

But such a mindset alone will not be enough. To allow this openness and dialogue to flourish, not merely at corporate level between the CEO and the key executives, but throughout the company, an infrastructure and management process has to be designed and maintained. Indeed, ultimately such openness and dialogue are yet another invaluable 'resource' for the company's managers, enabling them constantly to see clearly where things stand; for example, what precisely constitutes 'success' and how well is the company progressing towards achieving it. This sort of information is clearly invaluable in helping managers to do their job. This 'resource', the infrastructure for transparency, can provide an accurate view of the true state of affairs in the workplace, often taking the form of an executive dialogue centre or virtual CEO office, which will usually bear the fingerprints of the company communications director.

Lessons learned

- As a rule, companies have their largest capability gap (the greatest misalignment) in transparent communication and decision making. This is why the communications director has to play a key role in establishing and maintaining a structured corporate dialogue.
- The importance of corporate dialogue means that the communications director has to generate effective interaction between the leadership team and the executive community to build the corporate story, and keep that interaction alive.
- A company's transparency and accountability can be significantly reinforced by opening it up to society at large through dialogue with outside stakeholders.
- The communications director has to bring the strategic alignment agenda to life and keep the corporate story vivid, using any kind of audiovisual means and various forms of interactive infrastructure.
- To be really successful, the communications director has to operate seamlessly with the CEO in supporting a pull and push management style through communication.

Epilogue

In our view, Charles Handy's article 'Balancing corporate power: A new federalist paper' is an important contribution to the search for a new system to govern large corporations.[1] He suggests trying to translate to the world of commerce the principles that have defined federations in the political world for over 200 years, in order to provide a governing and management framework for business.

He lists these principles as follows:

- *Subsidiarity* places power at the corporation's lowest point. This means that someone higher up in the organization should not take on responsibilities that actually belong to a subordinate.
- *Interdependence* spreads power around, avoiding the risk of central bureaucracy. Federalism encourages cooperation and synergies, but not centralization.
- A proper federation needs a *common language and currency* – a uniform way of doing business. A common budgeting system or a clear definition of profit would be corporate examples.
- *Separation of powers* keeps management, monitoring and governance in segregated units. Handy argues that when these functions are combined in one body, the short term will tend to drive out the long, with month-to-month management and monitoring stealing the time and attention needed for true governance.
- *Twin citizenship* ensures a strong federal presence in an independent region. This principle is particularly important in

corporations operating in multiple industries. One is both a member of one's business unit and of the company as a whole. Corporate values then spread across all businesses within one corporate environment.

At the end of his article, Handy writes: 'The assumptions behind federal thinking – and the empty space for individual initiatives – are that those higher up may not know better. That assumption requires a lot of trust.' He continues: 'Federalism reverses a lot of traditional management thinking. In particular, it assumes that most of the energy is out there, away from the top. Power, in federalist thinking, is redistributed because no one person and no one group can be all-wise, all-knowing, all-competent.' He concludes: 'Federalism is not simple. It matches complexity with complexity.'

Some ten years later, Peter Drucker stated boldly that the American record of top management performance suggested not human failure but system failure.[2] Does this mean that the thinking of people like Handy does not work? No. It is just that what he recommended couldn't be measured, and therefore couldn't be managed in a workable system.

We feel that we can learn much from the principles of federalism, but trust, openness and the many elements of complexity need to be embedded in a measurable system. Opening up the operational black box and managing by pull and push as well as instituting a true organization-wide dialogue may only have become possible in our digital age. Now we are able to manage strategic alignment more effectively by means of that dialogue. Our experience has shown one way to make these principles actionable. Finally, technology has adapted *to us* so we can apply great management thinking in a controlled way. We have reached the age of managing beyond control.

Appendix I
Gap Analyses

Top 10 Priorities and strengths Corporate Benchmark 2005

Areas of misalignment

Rank	Section	Category	Desired	Current	MM Gap
1	QC	Transparent Communication and Deision making	8.6	5.4	36
2	QC	Innovation	8.5	5.8	25
3	CO	Meritocracy	8.6	6.1	25
4	IO	Dynamic Industry Player	8.7	6.1	25
5	BR	Profit Sharing	8.1	5.4	25
6	QC	Clear Intent	8.8	6.3	25
7	PD	Career Ownership	8.5	5.9	24
8	QC	Customer Value-Creation	8.8	6.5	21
9	IO	Attractive Employer	8.9	6.6	21
10	QC	Continuous Improvement	8.5	6.1	20

Areas of alignment

Rank	Section	Category	Desired	Current	MM Gap
1	IO	Responsible Company	8.3	7.3	2
2	PE	Personal Accountability	8.6	7.4	2
3	QB	Trustworthy	9.2	8.2	2
4	QB	Influential	8.8	7.4	5
5	PE	Freedom to Act	8.7	7.3	6
6	QB	Management Competence	9.1	7.6	6
7	CO	Open to Partnerships	7.8	6.1	6
8	IO	Solid Reputation	8.4	6.9	6
9	QC	Result & Output Driven	8.4	6.9	8
10	CO	Shared Principles and Values	8.7	7.0	8

QC Quality of the company   CO Culture of the organization   IO Image of the organization
PE Personal Empowerment   PD Personal Development   BR Benifits & Rewards

The above chart is a report of the outcomes of an organizational capability scan, showing areas of Alignment and Improvement listed in descending order.

Note 1: Gaps range from 0 to 100 and are calculated from organizational scan scores by means of a proprietory formula.

Note 2: The scoring scale used for the MeyerMonitor organizational scan was modified in the second quarter of 2004. Results used in this book from prior to the modification have been re-figured for consistency with later results.

Appendix II
Campaign Invitations and Protocols

NUMICO

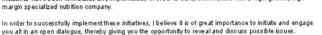

Dear Colleagues,

Welcome to the MeyerMonitor survey.

As you all know, 2003 has been a year of significant change in our company in which many strategic initiatives have been formulated and implemented in order to transform Numico into a high-growth, high-margin specialized nutrition company.

In order to successfully implement these initiatives, I believe it is of great importance to initiate and engage you all in an open dialogue, thereby giving you the opportunity to reveal and discuss possible issues.

The MeyerMonitor survey will provide us with insight into the alignment of our organization with our strategy. The monitor enables you to assess our current performance on various aspects of our organization and also communicate your ambitions for the company. In doing the assessment, please focus on your immediate work environment of the organization.

Based on the outcomes of last year's survey we have started some important initiatives on Communication, People and Values. During our meeting in June we will discuss the results of these initiatives.

The MeyerMonitor process is completely anonymous. None of the parties involved is able to link individual scores to you personally or to a group of participants smaller than 5 people. This means that you can be completely frank in your assessment.

Your input is crucial to help build an organization that is even better equipped to make the strategy happen.

Kind regards,

Jan Bennirk

Sara Lee H&BC Chat session

CHAT RULES / CONDUCT / INSTRUCTIONS

Chat with Vincent Janssen: please read the page below before entering the chat.

Protocol
The purpose of the chat with Vincent Janssen is to offer Sara Lee H&BC colleagues worldwide the possibility to share their view on Project Focus, the outcomes of the survey and to generate new ideas directly with Vincent Janssen.

Vincent Janssen himself will structure the session, introduce the topics, ask questions, explain discuss and answer questions you might have. Please be open and challenge each other on the arguments being discussed. Finally, always take the improvement of Sara Lee H&BC as starting point of the discussion. Our overall goal is to make Project Focus a long-lasting success.

The chat session with Vincent Janssen is an **un-moderated** chat. This means that all your input, after you click "SEND" or press "ENTER" twice, will be immediately visible to all participants.

In order to maintain some order in the discussion, you are asked not to submit of-topic input during a discussion. **Please read the contributions of others before you submit your text and focus on Vincent Janssen's specific question, which is visible all the time.**

During the chat session Bernt Smit accompanies Vincent Janssen. He is also available to answer any of your questions. If you reply to a message from another participant than Vincent Janssen, please include the name of the person you are speaking to in the text field.

Due to the large numbers of participants and viewers in the chat, Vincent Janssen may not be able to answer all your questions or respond to all your contributions. Therefore a transcript and summary of the chat will be produced after the 10th of March.

Please click the "LOGOFF" button if you wish to exit the chat session.

Moderation

If too many people submit their input at the same time (everyone is speaking at the same time) a moderator will intervene and turn on moderation to structure the discussion.

Moderation means that your input will be submitted to the moderator first. The moderator accepts only those entries that contribute to a structured discussion. Only after acceptance your contributions appear in the chat screen.

Please do not be offended if your entries are not chosen by the moderator to be shown in the chat screen – your input will be included in the transcript and Vincent Janssen may want to reply to them by e-mail the week after the chat session.

Appendix III
A Case Study on
Measuring – ABN AMRO

On 20 May 2000, Rijkman Groenink was appointed ABN AMRO managing board chairman. He used his inaugural address to expound his strategic vision for the bank. It began with a clear, measurable goal: to be in the top five of an international group of 20 'peer banks' based on total return to shareholders. This announcement turned the focus of the bank's value system squarely back to creating value for the shareholders. Pleasing shareholders would also ease the transition among bank employees from fearing for their own futures, within an organization vulnerable to outside predators, to a healthy sense of shared risk.

Groenink also took the opportunity to announce the second element of his change strategy: a restructuring of the bank's organization. Before 2000, ABN AMRO had operated mainly under a matrix structure in which managers were responsible to both functional and country superiors. Many people within the organization felt that this tended to blur lines of responsibility and so lessen accountability. Now accountability would be more important than ever, in light of the greater autonomy that was being granted to lower-level managers to do whatever they thought necessary to get closer to the consumer and to create economic value added for the bank. The current 'universal banking' structure – i.e. offering all

Table A.1 Sample results from ABN AMRO organizational capability scan (a gap of 0 means full alignment; a gap of 100 means total misalignment)

	ABN TOTAL GAP	INV BANK GAP
Continuous improvement	48	72
Result & output driven	39	72
Transparent communication & decision making	59	79
Direct and action oriented	33	53
Meritocracy	40	66
Good financial package	16	33

banking services – tried unsuccessfully to be all things to all people and was now to be firmly refocused on distinct banking operations. In parallel with this, there would be a drastic shrinking of the 'corporate centre'.

At the age of 51, Groenink had been promoted from inside to the position of CEO. He was well aware of the bank's problems: the muddled lines of authority and responsibility; the stagnating financial returns; and the all-too-widespread tolerance of mediocrity. He had some principles of his own that he was determined to push forward in this new leadership position. Among these was a strong belief in accountability, together with much greater openness within the organization.

During the first three months of 2000, Groenink had been working with his newly formed Managing Board analysing the past, drawing conclusions about the present and agreeing on a new strategy and a new organizational structure for the future. With his approaching accession to chairman, he expected that the Board's assessment would probably be shared by the majority of senior managers, and so would reveal the lack of executional capability for the bank as a whole. He decided to carry out an organizational capability scan involving 329 members of the bank's top ranks – senior vice-presidents, executive vice-presidents and senior executive vice-presidents, in addition to all members of the Managing Board. This would be a clear demonstration of his personal commitment to greater openness and dialogue. There was a risk involved, of course.

What if the scan discovered that opinion throughout the upper executive ranks wanted to take the bank in another direction entirely, or saw no need for any sort of changes at all – even in the face of clearly unacceptable performance for shareholders?

As it turned out, the results did demonstrate a broad base of support for change. High gaps on issues like Meritocracy, Continuous Improvement, Result and Output Driven and Transparent Communication (see Table A.1) showed clearly that senior managers wanted something better than what the current ABN AMRO organization was offering. There was another interesting aspect of the results: the stark differences reported between different subsets of bank personnel. These differing results held an important lesson for the bank's new leadership as they developed their change campaign.

Appendix IV
A Case Study on Matching – Numico

When Jan Bennink became CEO of Numico (www.numico.com) in May 2002, the company was under significant pressure. In the late 1990s, Numico had expanded into the vitamin business in the US by acquiring Rexall Sundown and SGNC stores and this decision had turned out to be problematic. Financial performance had suffered, while Numico's core businesses (baby food and clinical food) had also started to decline. Bennink decided to shake up the company by replacing the entire executive board and many senior managers, restructuring the company into five divisions, selling the vitamin businesses if they didn't improve quickly, and – his first move – averting a cash crisis by securing lines of credit with a consortium of banks.

In June 2003, as soon as the new executive board was complete, Bennink arranged for a senior managers' meeting with the objective

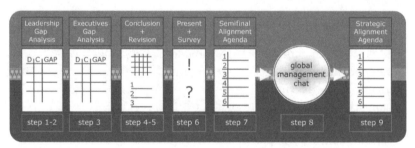

Figure A.1 The matching process: preparing the Strategic Alignment Agenda

Table A.2 (Step 4) Conclusions of misalignment

- **'Information and Knowledge Sharing' (MM Gap 59)**
  - *'Transparency of Communication and Decision Making'*
  - *'Access to Knowledge'*

- **'Innovation' (MM Gap 48)**
  - *'Reinvent for Growth'*
  - *'Continuous Improvement'*
  - *'Customer Value Creation'*
  - *'Adaptive and Open to Change'*

- **'External Image' (MM Gap 48)**
  - *'Dynamic Industry Player'*
  - *'Attractive Employer'*
  - *'Positive Media Profile'*

- **'Promote for Performance' (MM Gap 39)**
  - *'Employee Value Creation'*
  - *'Assessment and Feedback'*
  - *'Meritocracy'*
  - *'Career Ownership'*
  - *'Professional development'*

- **'Rewards' (MM Gap 33)**
  - *'Good Financial Package'*
  - *'Lifestyle Benefits'*
  - *'Compensation Based on Contribution'*

of introducing the new team, explaining the new strategy, energizing people, 'reconnecting with the managers' and signing off on the strategic alignment agenda (Step 8 in Figure A.1). As Bennink remarked at the time: 'I had to make decisions fast to save the company. Then you don't have much time to consult with managers in the business. That is a matter of priority.'

In preparation for this managers' conference, Bennink wanted to 'take the pulse' of his organization, and so ran an organizational capability scan among his top 200 people. 'Now that the basics are

Table A.3 (Step 9) The strategic alignment agenda

> 1. Transparency of communication and decision making.
> 2. People development.
> 3. Company values.

back in place, it is time to work on improving the organizational capabilities, the way we do things', he maintained (Step 3).

The survey revealed that the organization was much less aligned than the benchmark sample of peer companies and this provided Bennink with an urgent mandate for change. The key outcomes revealed misalignment on the areas shown in Table A.2 (Step 4).

From this, the board's strategic initiatives were re-defined as:

1   Align the business behind a strategy aimed at high growth and high margins.
2   Create a transparent organization with clear accountabilities.
3   Reduce working capital.

This led to a focus on three key capability improvement issues, which were discussed at the managers' meeting and resulted in the strategic alignment agenda shown in Table A.3 (Step 9).

In discussion groups, the top 200 managers developed project proposals around these three themes and presented them to the board. At this session, Jan Bennink and his executive team commented on the plans, decided which would be discarded immediately and assigned board members as project sponsors for the retained plans. Project teams worked on these organizational improvement projects in the ensuing months.

At the managers' meeting in June 2004, Bennink took the opportunity to conduct another organizational capability scan to check on his company's progress. He remarked: 'Doing a survey process like we did with MeyerMonitor provides you with a language system – in fact a structured dialogue around improving the organizational capabilities'. 2004 and 2005 showed a further strengthening of both Numico's strategic alignment as well as its financial results.

Appendix V
A Case Study on Managing –
Sara Lee/DE

Sara Lee/DE is an example of a company that over a period of four years has consistently managed the improvement of its four strategic capabilities.

In 2000, Sara Lee/DE was faced with two issues: on the one hand, an urge to leave local companies as free and entrepreneurial as possible; and on the other, a perceived need to strengthen the corporate image, as well as a financial requirement to streamline operations and create synergies between local subsidiaries with often quite different ways of working.

During the spring of 2000, Herman Bouwman – executive board member and responsible for talent alignment – examined the data coming from the company's organizational capability scan. Inside the operating arena, the following four areas of misalignment inspired him to take specific measures:

- The image of the organization:
  - Dynamic industry player (gap score 50)
  - Attractive employer (gap score 40)
- Organizational openness:
  - Transparent communication and decision making (gap score 50)

- Employee development:
  - Employee value creation (gap score 46)
- Work–life balance:
  - Work–life balance (gap score 35)

Transforming the corporate image

The capability data revealed a particularly wide gap when it came to 'Attractive Employer'; clearly, there was a unstated sense of frustration within the organization over its inability to recruit high-quality talent. Further investigation duly disclosed that both internal and external factors were involved. Yes, Sara Lee/DE's image as a place to work among university and business school students was generally eclipsed by other firms, but in addition the company's internal posture towards recruitment also varied widely from division to division, from the recruitment methods and policies used by the various business units to the training they could promise new employees once they were hired.

Table A.4

	GAP 2000	GAP 2001	GAP 2002	GAP 2003
Dynamic industry player	50	46	37	28
Attractive employer	40	26	21	18

Table A.5

	GAP 2000	GAP 2001	GAP 2002	GAP 2003
Transparent communication & decision making	50	38	33	31

Fortunately, all these problems could be addressed institutionally. The efforts at Sara Lee/DE both to burnish the company's outside image and to standardize and optimalize internal recruitment practices have borne fruit not only in a greater supply of high-quality new talent, but also in the data of subsequent organizational capability scans. (Table A.4).

Opening up the company internally

The scan showed that managers wanted to be better informed (Table A.5). In particular, the comments revealed that they wanted more openness about their own evaluation and professional development processes. The result was several new improvement initiatives, varying from a better-functioning intranet to an online management review system.

Development

Company efforts to create a system of professional development that was more attractive to its executives, centred around a significant

Table A.6

| | GAP | GAP | GAP | GAP |
	2000	2001	2002	2003
Employee value creation	46	35	27	31

Table A.7

| | GAP | GAP | GAP | GAP |
	2000	2001	2002	2003
Work-life balance	35	20	23	28

upgrading of its 'Learning Site'. It was transformed from little more than a standard company-wide intranet for top- and mid-level managers into a comprehensive information-window which enabled personnel to keep close track of their present with the company (e.g. salary, vacation days, benefits, performance reviews) and their future (e.g. training, promotion opportunities). This new communication- and personnel-management system enabled Sara Lee/DE to shift the focus in its relations with those executives away from a preoccupation with compensation towards helping them further develop the skills they needed to succeed, and so help the company succeed (Table A.6).

Work–life balance

Many of the participants in the scan expressed concern about their work duties impinging more and more on their private lives. Although by its very nature this problem demanded a local approach, no subsidiary was left on its own to solve it. Instead, best practices were shared (e.g. flexitime, international training starting on Mondays instead of Sundays, etc.). For the last two years, management has accepted that they can live with gaps in a range between 25 and 30 (Table A.7).

Sara Lee International

As part of a major transformation in 2005, Sara Lee-De was renamed Sara Lee International. To ensure strategic alignment during the transformation, Sara Lee Corporation decided to measure all its businesses worldwide. Additionally, the company's new CEO, Brenda Barnes started, as part of the managing process, to use structured chat sessions to maintain an ongoing dialogue with her most senior management around the globe.

Appendix VI
How Aligned Is Your Company?

To receive a real-time initial score and overview of the strategic alignment status of your company, visit the 'Beyond Control' website: www.beyondcontrol.info.

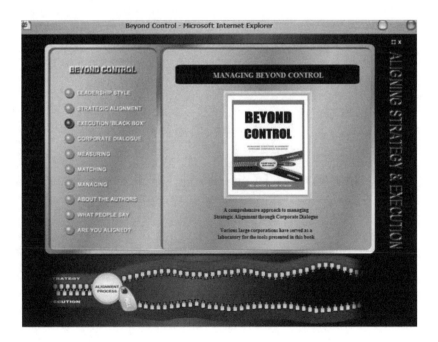

On this site you will find a shortened TransCountability survey, which will enable you to obtain a brief overview of your company's capacity for strategic alignment. Then this is quantified in a *capacity for alignment index* derived from the full organizational capability model. Specifically, the index is calculated on the basis of seven out of the 39 categories of the operating arena, namely categories pertaining to four questions linked to the four factors determining strategic alignment capacity.

These factors involve: (1) strategic intent; (2) objectives; (3) interaction; and (4) managerial support. The *capacity for alignment index* aggregates them into a single calculation. This must attain a certain value (globally benchmarked) for sufficient transparency and accountability to exist within the organization and therefore to make alignment possible. Such an organization is termed 'TransCountable'.

Notes

Introduction

1 Although throughout the book we have used the pronoun 'he' in preference to the more cumbersome 'he or she', this is in no way intended to suggest we believe that all managers or CEOs are male.

2 Throughout the book we have used real-life MeyerMonitor data. We emphasize that the conclusions drawn from these data are the authors' alone.

Chapter 1

1 'Earn-out provisions' are sometimes used when one company acquires another and involve, in addition to the agreed purchase-price for the acquired company, the possibility of an additional amount of money (a 'premium') being paid to the acquired company's owners if that company, now operating as a subsidiary of the acquiring company, achieves certain well-defined financial targets. Generally, the premium is calculated to reflect the acquired company's future profitability, and its purpose is mainly to ensure that its owners remain and continue to work in its long-term interest, and therefore in the long-term interest of the combined firm.

Chapter 2

1 This look at the development of corporations during the last several decades draws heavily on an article in the *Economist*, 'The way ahead', November 1, 2001.

2 Sydney Finkelstein (2003), *Why Smart Executives Fail*, London: Portfolio.

3 Data from our Organizational Capability research database, described later in this book.

4 *BusinessWeek*, April 9, 2001.

5 C. Montgomery and R. Kaufman, 'The board's missing link', *Harvard Business Review*, March 2003.

6 Data: Securities & Exchange Commission, *BusinessWeek*, March 24, 2003.

Chapter 4

1 'Tyrants, statesmen and destroyers', *Fortune*, November 18, 2002.

2 Interview with Clifton Leaf, 'Temptation is all around us', *Fortune*, November 18, 2002.

Chapter 7

1 Roland Kupers, 'What organisational leaders need to know about the new science of complexity', *Complexity*, Vol. 6, No. 1, 2000.

2 Erick Beinhocker (1997), 'Strategy at the Edge of Chaos', *The McKinsey Quarterly*, 1997 Number 1, pp. 38–39.

3 Charles Handy, *The Empty Raincoat*, Hutchinson, London, 1994.

4 Morton Bremer Maerli, 'Den som intet våger . . . ' [He who does not venture . . .; article in Norwegian], hyperlink: http://www.apollon.uio.no/vis/art/1996/3/dens.

5 Niklas Luhmann and Rhodes Barrett, *Risk: A Sociological Theory*, Aldine de Gruyter, Berlin, 1993.

Chapter 8

1 Robert McNamara, *HBS Alumni Bulletin*, September, 2004.

2 All of this would meet *Fortune*'s suggestions in the article 'Why companies fail' (May 2002) and its advice on turning employees into corporate governors.

Chapter 9

1 This is expressed as the 'operating arena' in this book.

Chapter 10

1 March 17, 2003.

2 Walker information/Hudson Institute, *Global Employee Relations Report*, 2000.

3 Now part of Pfizer Inc.

4 Ivo Smit (Kellogg, MBA Class of 2000): 'The MM career monitor provided me with insight into my priorities and helped me find a company where my ambitions were in line with their performance. In addition, it enabled me to ask more in-depth questions during the interview on the quality of the organization I was applying to.'

Epilogue

1 Charles Handy, 'Balancing corporate power: A new federalist paper', *Harvard Business Review*, Nov–Dec 1992.

2 Peter Drucker, 'The way ahead', *Economist*, November 1, 2001.

Index